(A GOLDEN HANDBOOK OF COLLECTIBLES)

# Carnival Glass

GERALDINE COSENTINO

REGINA STEWART

Golden Press • New York
Western Publishing Company, Inc.
Racine, Wisconsin

# Acknowledgments

The authors wish to express their appreciation to the individual collectors who granted permission to photograph pieces from their private collections to illustrate the examples used in this book. The pieces photographed are from the private collections of: Salvatore Aartsma, Marilyn A. Anderson, Marina Dusé, Vivienne S. Lang, Charles Marootian, and Modesta Saveriana. Grateful acknowledgment is also made to the following for their generous help in checking and researching: Salvatore Aartsma; Robert Wagner; Sherman Hand, author of *Colors in Carnival Glass*; A. R. Marks, Director of Public Relations, Wheaton Industries, Millville, New Jersey; The L. E. Smith Glass Company, Mount Pleasant, Pennsylvania; Phill Bee, Marketing Department, Anchor Hocking Corporation, Lancaster, Ohio; Helen Warner, Customer Service Dept., The Fenton Art Glass Company, Williamstown, West Virginia; and Lucile J. Kennedy, Sales Manager, Imperial Glass Corporation, Bellaire, Ohio.

ART DIRECTOR: Remo Cosentino
DESIGN: Elizabeth Alexander
PHOTOGRAPHY: John Garetti

Library of Congress Catalog Card Number: 76-406

Copyright © 1976 by Western Publishing Company, Inc. All rights reserved, including the rights of reproduction and use in any form or by any means, including the making of copies by any photo process, or by any electronic or mechanical device, printed or written or oral, or recording for sound or visual reproduction or for use in any knowledge retrieval system or device, unless permission in writing is obtained from the copyright proprietor. Printed in the U.S.A. Published by Golden Press, New York, N.Y.

GOLDEN, GOLDEN PRESS®, and GOLDEN HANDBOOK are trademarks of Western Publishing Company, Inc.

# Contents

| | |
|---|---|
| **INTRODUCTION** | 4 |
| **HISTORY** | 7 |
| **COLOR AND PATTERN** | 16 |
| **SHAPES** | 25 |
|    VASES | 26 |
|    BOWLS | 39 |
|    BOWLS ON MATCHING STANDS | 55 |
|    FOOTED BOWLS | 57 |
|    COMPOTES | 65 |
|    ROSEBOWLS | 67 |
|    NAPPIES | 68 |
|    BONBONS | 71 |
|    TABLE SETS | 72 |
|    WATER SETS | 74 |
|    TUMBLERS | 77 |
|    BOTTLES | 78 |
|    PLATES | 83 |
|    BASKETS | 84 |
|    HATS | 87 |
|    CANDLESTICKS | 87 |
|    HATPINS | 90 |
|    MISCELLANEOUS | 93 |
|    INSULATORS | 94 |
| **LATER IRIDIZED GLASS** | 97 |
| **NEW CARNIVAL GLASS** | 105 |
| **COLLECTING AND PURCHASING** | 116 |
| **CARE AND DISPLAY** | 120 |
| **GLOSSARY** | 122 |
| **BIBLIOGRAPHY** | 124 |
| **INDEX** | 125 |

# Introduction

At one time the United States was a nation of craftsmen producing one-of-a-kind items for the decorative and utilitarian needs of our homes. With the coming of the Industrial Revolution we moved away from this handicraft tradition to factory-made products which were still influenced by the original craftsmen and artisans of the past. This mass production made many luxury items available to the average home at the turn of the century. One of these was the decorative, iridescent glassware known today as Carnival glass.

Carnival glass is a colored, pressed glassware with a fired-on iridescent finish made in the United States from about 1905 to 1925. It was originally intended as an inexpensive substitute for the costly hand-blown iridescent Victorian Art glass, produced by, among others, Tiffany and Carder. Owning sets of decorative Carnival glass became very fashionable; water pitchers with matching tumblers, table sets, and punch bowls with matching cups were especially desirable. Compotes, baskets, and vases were also popular as ornaments for the home.

Most of the Carnival glass produced was made by four companies. They were the Fenton Art Glass Company of Williamstown, West Virginia, the Imperial Glass Company of Bellaire, Ohio, the Millersburg Glass Company of Millersburg, Ohio, and the Northwood Glass Company of Wheeling, West Virginia.

This decorative iridescent glassware wasn't originally called Carnival glass. The name came into use after the 1920s, when the glass was used as prizes at carnivals and fairs.

This was a period of decline in the history of Carnival glass. It remained hidden in basements and attics until, years later, it began to attract the attention of collectors who were drawn to the rich variety of its colors, shapes, and patterns.

Antiques, increasingly rare and expensive, have become the province of the knowledgeable few who have both the time and the money to spend on their collections. In order to enjoy owning Carnival glass it is not necessary to emulate this type of collector. What is necessary is an informed approach to collecting.

One of the purposes of this book is to give the beginning collector just that. It is an introduction and a guide for those who would like to know more about this fascinating glassware. Many of the well-known patterns, shapes, and colors have been illustrated. In addition, chapters on recognizing and collecting later iridized glass and New Carnival glass (contemporary pieces and reproductions of the original Carnival ware) have been included for those who may enjoy owning these other types of iridescent glassware—and to help eliminate some of the confusion that exists in this new area of collecting. Information on care and display, as well as purchasing tips, has also been included.

Although Carnival glass has risen in price today, as have many of the other collectibles, we have not attempted to indicate the price of any of the pieces. A price guide quickly becomes dated, and tends to establish prices which are not realistic.

We are still a comparatively short distance away in time from the era in which this particular type of Americana was produced, yet we seek examples of these collectibles as eagerly today as the antiquarian of years ago sought his rarities. This reflects a changing trend in collecting; the desire for ownership of the individual centuries-old antique has given way to interest in owning the rich, varied, mass-produced items of our recent past.

# History

The nineteenth century was a time of change and progress in the United States. With the advent of the Industrial Revolution came the steam engine, the factory system, and mass production. Transportation improved, and by 1900 two hundred thousand miles of railroad track existed. Manufactured goods could now be carried farther and at a lower cost. Communications systems improved with the use of the telephone. Machines could do the work of individual craftsmen. This mechanization developed markets for inexpensive products. Retail distribution on a large scale became a reality.

New products, made by machine, were created for these new markets. The decorative arts became more elaborate, and design elements were now borrowed from all historical periods, for novelty became typical of the design of the late nineteenth century. The cult of the picturesque developed.

The 1880s and 1890s saw a renewed interest in Orientalism. Moorish decor was used in dens, libraries, and gentlemen's smoking rooms. Oriental rugs, Japanese and Chinese porcelains, lacquerware, and Japanese prints were popular. The middle class had begun to collect.

Glass has always been a popular collectible. Made of silica in the form of sand, and alkalis such as potash and carbonate of soda or lime, the mixture is brought to extreme heat in furnaces where the alkalis cause the fusion of the materials, and glass is created. This glass mixture is then shaped in one of three ways: it

---

Facing page: This well-executed design was a popular Northwood pattern. See **Three Fruits** (*Northwood*), page 62.

can be blown, molded, or pressed. The great bulk of the glassware produced in the nineteenth and twentieth centuries was machine-made pressed glass.

## PRESSED GLASS

Pressed glass was primarily an American invention. Pressing glass consists of forcing molten glass into shape under pressure. A plunger presses the glass into a mold from which the piece is then removed in an almost finished state. The interior of the mold is shaped like the exterior of the glassware. Most molds have two or more sections so that they can be taken apart after the glass is shaped, and then reassembled for the next article. Faint ridges or seams are left on the glass from the mold. These are called mold marks.

The first pressed glass was of a simple nature: drinking glasses and goblets. The perfection of machines for pressing glass led to more elaborate patterns and shapes. The earliest designs were of a geometric type derivative of cut glass (glass decorated with patterns that have been cut into its surface). After the Civil War, fruit and flower patterns were popular, and during the late Victorian era designs became more naturalistic and sentimental. All kinds of articles were made of pressed glass: tableware, ornaments, tiles, lamps, chandeliers—a patent was even taken out for a pressed-glass coffin.

## HAND-BLOWN ART GLASS

Hand-blown Art glass was very expensive, and out of the reach of all but a few wealthy collectors. From 1885 to 1900 there were all kinds of experiments with this type of glass, for the manufacture of Art glass involved solving complex technical problems.

**Tiffany.** Louis Comfort Tiffany was trained as a painter, but started to experiment with glassmaking in New York in 1870. He developed a vibrant coloring method for stained glass windows. Next came a process which recaptured the iridescent colors of ancient glass. This iridescent Art glass was called Favrile. Tiffany was influenced in his work by Art Nouveau designs that became popular during the late nineteenth century.

**Carder.** Another noted glass designer and technologist was Frederick Carder, founder of the Steuben Glass Works in Corning, New York. He emigrated from England where he had worked for the well-known English glassmaker John Northwood. Carder also experimented with color effects in glass, and invented Aurene, an ornamental iridescent Art glass.

The iridescent Carder Aurene and the Tiffany Favrile were the forerunners of Carnival glass.

## CARNIVAL GLASS

American women loved colorful glassware for its ability to brighten dark Victorian rooms. When an inexpensive method of producing iridized glass became available, the housewife could indulge in having a few pieces while still being able to provide for the necessities of life.

Carnival glass imitated the iridescence of handblown Art glass in shapes that were both decorative and useful. Utilitarian items such as punch bowls, water sets, and table sets were inexpensively priced. Carnival glass was primarily decorative, and was originally known as New Venetian Art, Parisian Art, Aurora, and Art Iridescent. It was sold in china and glass shops and in general stores, and through mail-order catalogues. These catalogues were a good source of supply for Carnival glass. The buyer could order from the illustrated catalogue pages and know exactly what would be sent. Carnival glass was also used as containers for grocery products such as mustard and pickles. Tea companies, candy companies, and furniture stores offered pieces as premiums for purchasing their products.

Carnival glass was a bigger success than any of its manufacturers had anticipated. Not only was it produced for the American market, but great quantities were exported to England and other parts of Europe as well. Although a number of companies made Carnival ware, most of it was produced by the following four companies—Fenton, Imperial, Millersburg, and Northwood.

## THE FENTON ART GLASS COMPANY

The Fenton Art Glass Company of Williamstown, West Virginia, was founded in 1905 by Frank L. Fenton and his brother John, in Martin's Ferry, Ohio. Frank Fenton had decided to make designs for his own company rather than work as a designer and glassmaker for others, as he had previously done. At first, his company decorated glass shapes in the Martin's Ferry factory. Then, in order to manufacture their own glass, the company moved to Williamstown, West Virginia. By 1907 the new factory was in operation, and Carnival glass became their most popular product.

Jacob Rosenthal, a master glassworker, helped the Fentons to develop their line of Carnival glass. He had begun working with glass soon after the Civil War, and had developed his own secret formulas for colored glass.

Several different colors of iridescence were created by spraying secret mixtures of metallic salts on various colors of hot glass and then refiring the pieces. Their most distinctive color was cobalt blue. Fenton made highly textured pieces in all the popular Carnival glass shapes. Some famous Fenton patterns are Butterfly and Berry, and Persian Medallion, first advertised in 1910, and Orange Tree, first advertised in 1911.

At first Fenton produced many other forms of colored glassware as well, but from 1910 to 1920 most of their production was Carnival glass. Though they continued to manufacture other lines of glassware, they had discontinued their line of Carnival glass by 1921.

## THE IMPERIAL GLASS COMPANY

The Imperial Glass Company of Bellaire, Ohio, was founded by Edward Muhleman in 1902. In the first years of its operation the firm produced pressed glass

This massive punch bowl set is in one of Fenton's most popular patterns. See **Orange Tree** *(Fenton)*, page 55.

utilitarian items such as jars, lampshades, and drinking glasses.

Their iridescent Carnival glass line was introduced in 1910 and production continued until about 1924. Two of their best-known patterns are Lustre Rose and Imperial's Grape. Both patterns were made in great quantities and in many different shapes, sizes, and colors. Imperial's most famous color was called Helios, after the Greek god of the sun. The Helios pieces have a green base glass which is coated with a predominantly gold or silver iridescence. The company is still operating in Bellaire, Ohio, and was the first to start producing the New Carnival glass (reissues of old Carnival ware) in the early 1960s.

## THE MILLERSBURG GLASS COMPANY

In 1910, John Fenton left the Fenton Art Glass Company and, with his brother Robert, founded the Millersburg Glass Company of Millersburg, Ohio. Millersburg Carnival glass, called Rhodium Ware, is known for its brilliant iridescence and the clarity of its base glass by those who have seen authenticated pieces.

The Millersburg patterns were produced in a limited variety of shapes and colors. Most of the identification of Millersburg patterns and shapes has been done from shards, pieces of discarded and broken glass, dug from the site of the old Millersburg factory.

The company was said to have specialized in water sets, berry sets, punch bowls and cups, and table sets. Two pieces which are prized by collectors come from the Millersburg factory. They are the Courthouse bowl and the Cleveland Memorial tray. The Millersburg bowl was produced as a souvenir piece and given to special friends and employees of the company; it was never sold. Some of the Millersburg patterns were

---

Facing page: This rosebowl is in one of the many Carnival glass grape patterns. See **Grape Delight**, page 67.

Hobnail Swirl, Whirling Leaves, Diamond, and Nesting Swan.

The company soon went bankrupt, and the molds for the Millersburg patterns were supposedly destroyed and sold for scrap metal. If this is true, the pieces made by Millersburg can never be reproduced from the original molds.

## THE NORTHWOOD GLASS COMPANY

Harry Northwood came from a famous English glassmaking family. The son of John Northwood, Harry came to the United States before 1885. He worked for different glass firms as a designer and manager before opening his own company. In 1902 he started his company at Wheeling, West Virginia, making colored glass novelties, pressed tableware, colored glass with opalescent edges, and pressed clear glass decorated with gold.

In 1910 Harry Northwood began to produce Carnival glass. His names for this new iridescent product were Pompeian, Regal, Venetian, and Parisian Art. About this time he began to use his trademark, an N with a line under it in a circle.

The Northwood products were so attractive that they sold without much advertising; they offered quantity as well as quality at inexpensive prices. Northwood's most popular Carnival pattern was Northwood's Grape and Cable, which was also made in clear and Custard glass. Another bestseller was the Peacock at the Fountain. Northwood's heavily raised designs held the iridescence very well, and may have accounted for some of their popularity.

The Northwood Company manufactured Carnival glass from 1910 to 1918 when the demand for Carnival glass lessened. With the death of Mr. Northwood in 1923, the company was disbanded.

**Other companies.** A number of other glass companies also produced Carnival ware, among them the Cam-

These graceful patterns — **Stippled Flower** on the left (described on page 52) and **Four Flowers** on the right (see page 83) — are enhanced by their beautiful opalescent edges.

bridge Glass Company of Cambridge, Ohio, the Jenkins Glass Company of Kokomo, Indiana, the Heisey Glass Company of Newark, Ohio, and the Indiana Glass Company of Dunkirk, Indiana.

Like most decorative accessories, Carnival glass reflected the fashions of its time. By the 1920s, as Victorian styles gave way to the lighter, brighter colors and streamlined designs of modern decor, Carnival glass became less and less fashionable. Left with inventory to dispose of, manufacturers sold their remaining stock to carnivals, and to wholesale dealers who supplied novelties and prize items for bazaars, fairs, and charitable organizations. As its popularity declined, Carnival glass was put away and forgotten until the 1950s, when collectors rediscovered this fascinating glassware.

# Color and Pattern

Among the most striking characteristics of Carnival glass are its distinctive colors and sparkling iridescence. Expensive hand-blown Art glass had these qualities, too, but never before had a colored iridescent glassware been made for the mass market.

## COLOR

Color occurs naturally in glass depending upon the oxides in the basic mixture. The color varies from a light green to brown or amber shades. All other colors are artificially produced by adding metallic oxides as coloring agents to the glass formula. Variations in heat, length of time in the furnace, and the formulas used all affect the color of the glass.

**Base glass color.** When referring to the color of Carnival glass, the base glass color only is meant. This is the color of the glass before the iridescence is applied. To determine the base glass color, hold the glass up to a good light or sunlight and look through the base of the piece where there is usually no applied iridescence. This is the base glass color, which may appear very different from the iridized portions of the piece.

For convenience, the colors in Carnival glass can be divided into two main categories: bright colors and pastel colors. The bright colors are red, blue, green, purple, amethyst, amber, and marigold. The pastels are clear, white, clambroth, lavender, aqua, and smoky.

**Bright colors.** Red is the rarest of all Carnival colors. As made by Fenton and Imperial, it is a bright cherry red. This was the most expensive color to produce because gold or copper was used to obtain the color. The most popular blue was a deep cobalt blue. Blue is made

COLOR and PATTERN  **17**

**Coin Dot** bowl (see page 40) with green base glass color

by using copper or cobalt. The Fenton Company made a variety of cobalt blue that has an amber edge. Green, made with iron, is usually a slightly bluish emerald color. Northwood greens are more yellow. There are many shades of purple—from dark to a light purple called amethyst. If the amethyst has a predominantly red tone, it is called fiery amethyst. Amber has a distinct brown tone caused by carbon and nickel. Not as much amber was made as were the other colors.

Marigold is not a true base glass color since it was produced by an even coating of an orange-colored flashing on clear glass, followed by the iridescent spray. Marigold was the most popular color, and it is comparatively easy to find pieces in marigold because so much more of it was produced. Marigold can also be found on an amethyst base glass color.

Bright colors were preferred in Carnival glass, and

# 18 COLOR and PATTERN

**Smooth Rib** bowl (see page 51) with the pastel base glass color called clambroth

all the bright colors, with the exception of red, were made in quantity.

**Pastel colors.** Clear Carnival glass has a pastel iridescence but no color of its own. White is a clear glass that has been frosted before the iridescence is applied. Clambroth has a very pale yellow color. Lavender is a very light purple-tinted base glass with light iridescence. Aqua is a mixture of blue and green. It is often found shading into amber with an opalescent edge. Smoky is a light gray base glass.

## IRIDESCENCE

Carnival glass was given its iridescence by spraying each piece with metallic salts, refiring, and then recooling the piece. Different combinations of metals produced different effects. Bright base glass pieces were iridized with deeply shaded colors; the pastel base glass pieces were iridized with light pastel colors, usually light blues, pinks, and greens. Only one or two workers knew each company's formula for iridizing, and when they changed jobs they would take the formulas with them. This makes it almost impossible to identify a manufacturer according to the iridescence of the glass.

## PATTERN

Patterned glassware for the mass market was made possible by the invention and development of machines for processing glass during the early nineteenth century. Skilled pattern makers were in great demand as hundreds of different patterns came into existence. These designers took their patterns with them when they changed jobs, enabling the glass companies to copy the more well-known patterns from one another. The large companies that produced Carnival glass had also made the earlier pressed pattern glass, and many of the patterns and designs in Carnival glass were also found in clear and colored pressed glassware without the iridescent finish.

Pattern glass became heavily decorated toward the close of the nineteenth century, and the designs showed the influence of all historical periods and styles from the earliest simple classic designs to the elaborate patterns popular during the late Victorian era.

Carnival glass patterns may be divided into several basic categories: geometric, naturalistic, and ornamental.

**Geometric.** The geometric designs were created to imitate the hand-incised cut-glass techniques. Large and small motifs often were contrasted in the same piece to imitate the brilliance and the refractive qualities of the more expensive cut glass. These designs were called near-cut, and were most often made in marigold. Some of the more popular Carnival near-cut patterns are Fashion, Twins, Diamond Lace, and Star and File. These usually appeared as exterior patterns, with or without an interior pattern.

**Naturalistic.** The largest category of Carnival glass patterns is the naturalistic. These patterns included fruits, flowers, and plants, birds, animals, scenic motifs, and various combinations of these motifs.

Of the fruit patterns, the grape enjoyed the greatest popularity. The three most famous grape patterns are Northwood's Grape and Cable, Imperial's Grape, and Fenton's Grape and Cable, although there are many other grape patterns as well, such as Vintage, Grape Arbor, Grape Delight, and Grape Cluster. Other fruit patterns are Peach and Pear, Three Fruits, and Fenton's Cherry.

The flower and plant patterns are sometimes rendered realistically and sometimes in a stylized manner. Some of the realistic flower patterns are Northwood's Poppy, Imperial's Pansy, Lustre Rose, and Imperial's Open Rose. The more stylized patterns are Leaf Rays, Mayflower, Carnival Holly, Northwood's Leaf and Beads, and Scotch Thistle.

The Peacock, in the bird category, was probably the second most popular design motif, the grape being first. Northwood produced two of the finest peacock patterns: Peacock at the Fountain, and Peacock and Urn. Other bird patterns are Singing Birds, and Robin.

Animal patterns were never made in as great a quantity as the fruit and flower motifs. Two well-known animal patterns are Panther, and Stag and Holly.

Few patterns in Carnival glass can be called scenic. They are usually found on plates or shallow bowls, and feature landscapes, sometimes with a Dutch feeling, such as the Double Dutch pattern. The Nu-Art plates by Imperial and the Millersburg Courthouse bowl, both rarities, belong to the scenic group.

These photographs illustrate three basic Carnival glass pattern categories. Above left: **Open Rose** *(Imperial)*, page 46, is an example of a naturalistic pattern. Above right: **Persian Medallion** *(Fenton)*, page 51, illustrates an ornamental design. Below: **Fashion** *(Imperial)* creamer and sugar, page 72, is an example of a geometric near-cut motif.

**Ornamental.** The ornamental designs range from extremely simple, almost plain patterns with ribs or simple panels to more sophisticated designs such as scrolls, palmettes, hearts, lyres, peacock feathers, and combinations of these. Often they have a vaguely Oriental name or feeling, in keeping with the Oriental design influence of the 1890s. Fenton's Persian Medallion is a good example of this, as is Nippon. The simple patterns are Stippled Ray, Fine Rib, and Wide Panel, all common Carnival glass patterns found in bowls, vases, and compotes of almost every size.

## ATTRIBUTIONS

An important question to the collector of Carnival glass has always been when, where, and by whom was a specific piece made: the question of attribution. The only company known to have marked most of their pieces was Northwood. Attributions of unmarked pieces made by Northwood, Fenton, Millersburg, Imperial, and other companies are based on previous

This footed banana bowl displays an outstanding lustre. The interior pattern is **Thistle** *(Fenton)*, described on page 62.

research by authorities well known in the field of Carnival glass. Much of the research into attributions was done by checking company records and the original advertisements of the Carnival glass companies.

The Northwood company had a variety of marks: a circle, an N with a dash underneath, and a combination of these two—an N in a circle, and an N with two circles around it. However, not all Northwood pieces are marked. It is quite possible to find two identical pieces of Northwood, one marked and the other unmarked. The Northwood mark could have worn away or been omitted from the unmarked piece. Familiarizing yourself with typical Northwood patterns helps to make accurate attributions possible.

There are certain characteristics which help in identifying pieces made by the Fenton company. There is a definite Fenton edge. It is a continuous series of rounded scallops alternating with smaller and more pointed flutes. This edge, usually combined with a smooth, iridized exterior, indicates a Fenton product. The Fenton Company also made a shade of cobalt blue with a reddish iridescence that causes the edge to appear amber.

When trying to identify the maker of a popular pattern, the presence of a secondary pattern often helps. For instance, Basketweave, Thumbprint, or Plume and Snowflake used on the exterior of a piece would indicate Northwood; Persian Medallion or Bearded Berry as a secondary pattern indicates that the piece in question was from the Fenton Company.

These guidelines to attribution apply to old Carnival glass only, and cannot be used to identify the New Carnival glass. The Fenton Art Glass Company now owns the old Northwood molds, and the Imperial Glass Company owns the original Heisey and Cambridge Glass Company molds. Both Fenton and Imperial are reproducing old glass under their new trademarks.

 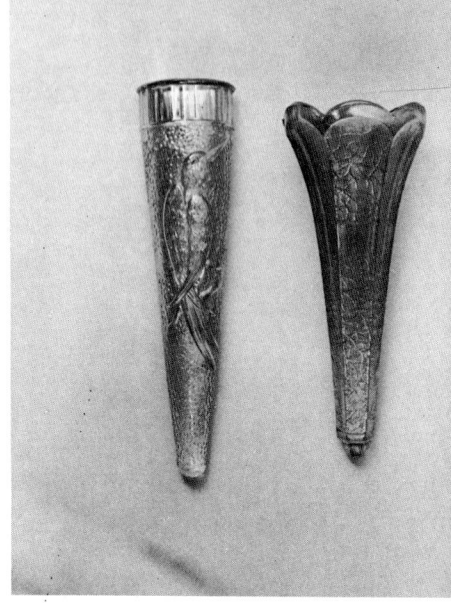

Carnival glass vases were produced in a variety of standard and unusual shapes. Above left: **Thin Rib** *(Northwood)*, page 36; **Fine Rib Fan**, page 30; **Beauty Bud**, page 26. Above right: **Woodpecker** wall vase, page 36; **Crackle** car vase, page 29.

The popular **Imperial's Grape** pattern, illustrated below, was made in many different shapes, sizes, and colors. Also see pages 43 and 76.

# Shapes

Carnival glass was first manufactured in decorative shapes such as vases and bowls. These proved to be so popular that manufacturers soon started producing other household items as well. Water sets were the most widely made, followed by table sets, punch bowls, and berry and ice cream sets. Dresser sets with matching cologne bottles, powder jars, dresser trays, pin trays, and hatpin holders were produced. Lamps, paperweights, mugs, ferneries, beads, and spitoons were made of Carnival glass. Advertising items and souvenir pieces were made to commemorate special events and companies.

The pieces illustrated here are a small selection from the great variety of shapes and patterns that exist in Carnival glass. They are representative of the most popular, well-known, and available items that can be purchased. It is not possible to give complete listings of which patterns were made in what colors and shapes. Very often a pattern shown did come in other shapes and colors. And it is also possible to find pieces which are similar but not exact in all details; because many molds were used throughout the production of a piece, slight variations may be found.

The sizes and colors listed in the pattern descriptions relate to the pieces photographed only. When a manufacturer's name is given, the particular piece photographed has been attributed to that maker (this does not necessarily mean that it is an exclusive pattern).

Most of the pattern names used follow the terminology of Marion Hartung, author of numerous volumes on Carnival glass, whose pattern names have become standard in this field.

# Vases

Vases were among the most popular shapes made in Carnival glass. Intended for decorative use, they were made in a wide variety of patterns, sizes, and colors.

Usually, vases had an allover pattern not often found on other shapes. These patterns range from heavily ornate designs to very plain ones. When a pattern was elongated to adjust to the length of the vase, it is called pulled out. The longer the vase, the more "pulled" the center pattern appears. Sometimes the vase has been twisted as it was pulled so that the pattern appears slightly turned.

Vases were made in heights from about six to twenty-two inches, the most popular height being from ten to twelve inches. There are different types of rims: flames, scallops, ruffles, flutes, and smooth. On the bases can be found multi-pointed stars, near-cut motifs, or petaled flowers. Other bases are simply smooth or slightly domed.

Vases are found in all the Carnival glass colors. However, not all patterns are found in every color.

**Beaded Bull's-eye**  Height: 8 inches. Base glass color: purple. Base: twenty-point star. (See page 33.)

Six vertical panels of bull's-eyes surrounded by beads are separated by very fine ribbing. As the bull's-eyes conform to the shape of the vase, they become extremely elongated.

**Beauty Bud**  Height: 9 inches. Base glass color: marigold on clear. Base: slightly domed foot. (See page 24.)

This small bud vase has nine panels. Three tiny twig-textured handles protrude from the foot, which is similarly textured.

---

Facing page: **Tree Trunk** (*Northwood*), page 36; **Rustic** (*Fenton*), page 35; **Hobnail Swirl** (*Millersburg*), page 30

| | |
|---|---|
| **Crackle** | Height: 7½ inches. Base glass color: marigold on clear. Base: pointed. (See page 24.)
Said to come from an old Hudson auto, this unusual car vase has a smooth band where it fits into a metal holder which was attached to the walls of the car. The six panels, which are curved at the top, are in the Crackle pattern. |
| **Diamond Point** *(Northwood)* | Height: 6 inches. Base glass color: green. Base: smooth. Northwood mark.
Height: 10¼ inches. Base glass color: marigold on amethyst. Base: smooth. Northwood mark.
This fine diamond pattern has a raised point forming the center of each diamond. |
| **Diamond Point and Fine Rib** | Height: 7 inches. Base glass color: marigold on amethyst. Base: twenty-point star.
Three diamond-point panels alternate with three fine rib panels. |
| **Fine Rib** | Height: 11½ inches. Base glass color: cobalt blue. Base: slightly domed. (See page 31.)
Narrow vertical ribs end in six arches, top and bottom. Six pulled flames form the rim of this popular design. The Fine Rib pattern cannot be definitely attributed to the Northwood Company unless it has been marked. |
| **Fine Rib** *(Northwood)* | Height: 9½ inches. Base glass color: deep purple. Base: smooth. Northwood mark. (See page 31.)
Height: 7 inches. Base glass color: marigold on clear. Base: smooth. Northwood mark. (See page 31.)
The Northwood vase is similar to the unmarked version described above. |

---

Facing page: **Diamond Point and Fine Rib; Diamond Point** *(Northwood),* **Diamond Point** *(Northwood)*

## VASES

**Fine Rib Fan** — Height: 8 inches. Base glass color: marigold on clear. Base: footed. (See page 24.)

This vase takes its name from its unusual fan shape. Fine ribs pattern three-quarters of the vase, up to the smooth rim.

**Hobnail** — Height: 9 inches. Base glass color: marigold on clear. Base: twenty-four-point star. (See page 33.)

Height: 11½ inches. Base glass color: marigold on clear. Base: thirty-point star. (See page 33.)

There are six panels of five hobnails each, separated by a rib which ends in the center of each pulled flame at the rim. The bottom of the larger Hobnail vase has a slight twist.

**Hobnail Swirl (Millersburg)** — Height: 10 inches. Base glass color: green. Base: thirty-two-point star. (See page 27.)

Raised hobnails are on a swirled background. This pattern has also been seen in cuspidors and rosebowls.

**Jack-in-the-Pulpit** — Height: 10 inches. Base glass color: marigold on clear. Base: sixteen-point star. (See page 32.)

The unusual shape of this vase is reminiscent of Tiffany Art glass. It has eight smooth panels separated by raised ribs which end in a teardrop effect.

**Knotted Beads** — Height: 9 inches. Base glass color: cobalt blue. Base: slightly domed. (See page 34.)

Strings of beads are on oval panels. There are four vertical rows of these ovals, with six ovals in each row. The rim is ruffled.

**Lined Lattice** — Height: 12 inches. Base glass color: deep purple. Base: nine feet. (See page 33.)

An unusual feature of the Lined Lattice vase is that

Above left: **Beaded Bull's-eye**, page 26. Above right: **Hobnail**, page 30; **Pulled Loop**, page 35; **Hobnail**, page 30

Facing page: **Jack-in-the-Pulpit**, page 30

Below left: **Lined Lattice**, page 30. Below right: **Sunflower Diamond** (Jenkins Glass Company), page 35

the pattern, formed by fine lines which come together and separate in leaflike shapes, extends down into nine feet, and up into nine pulled flames. This vase is heavily iridized both inside and out.

**Long Thumbprints** *(Fenton)* — Height: 11 inches. Base glass color: green. Base: near-cut star.

Four rows of thumbprints, nine around the base, become extremely elongated as they rise, ending in nine flames.

**Pulled Loop** — Height: 10¼ inches. Base glass color: marigold on amethyst. Base: thirty-point star. (See page 33.)

Each panel between the six raised ribs on this vase has five open loops.

**Ripple** *(Imperial)* — Height: 11½ inches. Base glass color: green. Base: twenty-point star.

This vase has both an interior and exterior pattern. The outer Ripple pattern consists of raised wavy horizontal lines; horizontal patterns such as this are unusual in vases. The interior pattern is Fine Rib.

**Rustic** *(Fenton)* — Height: 9 inches. Base glass color: marigold on clear. Base: domed foot. (See page 27.)

There are nine vertical rows of fifteen hobnails on a smooth background.

**Sunflower Diamond** *(Jenkins Glass Company)* — Height: 9 inches. Base glass color: marigold on clear. Base: eight-petaled daisy. (See page 33.)

Three panels of diamonds and sunflowers are separated by deeply indented lines. This vase displays an unusual combination: a raised near-cut pattern (the diamonds) and an indented pattern (the sunflower and leaves).

---

Facing page: **Ripple** *(Imperial)*; **Knotted Beads**, page 30; **Long Thumbprints** *(Fenton)*

## VASES

**Thin Rib**
*(Northwood)*

Height: 9 inches. Base glass color: marigold on clear. Base: thirty-two-point star. Northwood mark. (See page 24.)

Height: 11 inches. Base glass color: marigold and opalescent on clear. Base: thirty-two-point star. Northwood mark.

Height: 7½ inches. Base glass color: marigold on clear. Base: thirty-two-point star. Northwood mark.

The heavily raised ribs are evenly spaced and form the top of the vase. Thin Rib vases were made in large quantities and can only be attributed to Northwood if they are marked.

**Thin Rib Variant**
*(Northwood)*

Height: 11 inches. Base glass color: aqua. Base: four feet. Northwood mark.

Four ribs form four feet and four large flame tips on this vase. It has an amber iridescence and opalescent ribs.

**Tree Trunk**
*(Northwood)*

Height: 9½ inches. Base glass color: purple. Base: smooth. Northwood mark. (See page 27.)

Small hobnails are on a smooth background with curved markings giving the appearance of a textured tree trunk. The vase ends in nine flames.

**Woodpecker**

Height: 8¼ inches. Base glass color: marigold on clear. Base: pointed. (See page 24.)

A large bird on a textured background is shown on the curved front of this wall vase. The back of the vase is flat, with a hole about an inch down from the top edge. The hole was used for hanging the vase on a nail in the wall, or it could be threaded and hung with cord or ribbon.

---

Facing page: **Thin Rib** *(Northwood)*; **Thin Rib Variant** *(Northwood)*; **Thin Rib** *(Northwood)*

**Beads** *(Northwood)*, page 40

**Dragon and Lotus** *(Fenton)*, page 40

**Diamond Lace,** page 40

**Diamond Ring,** page 40

# Bowls

The largest variety of patterns is found in Carnival glass bowls. They came in sizes ranging from small sauce dishes to large punch bowls. They were round or oval, with a footed base, flat base, or matching stand. The most popular type was the shallow one, made in many diameters, patterns, and colors.

Within the general category of bowls can be found fruit bowls, orange bowls, banana bowls, berry bowls with individual matching sauce dishes, and nut bowls. Punch bowls came with matching cups, wire cup hangers, and stands.

Bowls often had two patterns, since the bowl shape lent itself to the most variation in pattern. Bowls can be found with an interior pattern distinctly different from the exterior, or with a different version of the interior pattern used as a secondary exterior pattern. When a bowl has only one pattern, its shape and intended use usually determined whether the pattern was placed on the interior or exterior. The unpatterned side was left smooth, with or without iridescence. Occasionally the pattern side was not iridized but the smooth side was.

Quite a variety of bases were used on Carnival glass bowls. Some bowls sat on smooth collar bases while others had three or four feet. The designs of the feet varied from very plain to textured and twig shaped, as well as the more classic scroll, and the ball-and-claw. There was also a spatulate foot which resembled a deep scallop of glass and usually carried some of the exterior pattern.

Most of the patterns found on Carnival glass bowls can also be found on the other shapes, except for commemorative designs or advertising pieces. These patterns and shapes were made in many colors, although each pattern may not have been made in all colors.

| | |
|---|---|
| **Beads**<br>*(Northwood)* | Diameter: 8 inches. Base glass color: green. Base: twenty-four-point star. Northwood mark. (See page 38, top left.)<br>Intersecting shapes made up of strips of beading are interspersed with stylized daisies on the exterior, which is not iridized. The Northwood mark is in the center of the smooth, iridized interior. |
| **Coin Dot** | Diameter: 7⅝ inches. Base glass color: green. Base: smooth collar.<br>The interior pattern of this bowl is one of raised, stippled dots on a smooth background. The dots become smaller as they go toward the center, which contains seven large dots. The exterior is smooth and iridized. |
| **Diamond Lace** | Diameter: 9 inches. Base glass color: purple. Base: near-cut star. (See page 38.)<br>The exterior of this handsome bowl is in the Diamond Lace near-cut pattern. The interior is smooth and iridized. |
| **Diamond Ring** | Diameter: 9 inches. Base glass color: marigold on clear. Base: near-cut. (See page 38.)<br>A typical near-cut pattern is on the exterior, while the interior is smooth and iridized. |
| **Dragon and Lotus**<br>*(Fenton)* | Diameter: 8¾ inches. Base glass color: cobalt blue. Base: smooth collar. (See page 38.)<br>An open lotus alternates with a dragon on the eight medallions on the interior of this heavily iridized bowl. Between each medallion is a closed, stemmed lotus. A ruffled ribbon twined with daisy and peacock feather motifs circles the center bottom. The exterior is smooth and iridized. |

---

Facing page: **Coin Dot.** (This pattern is illustrated in color on page 17.)

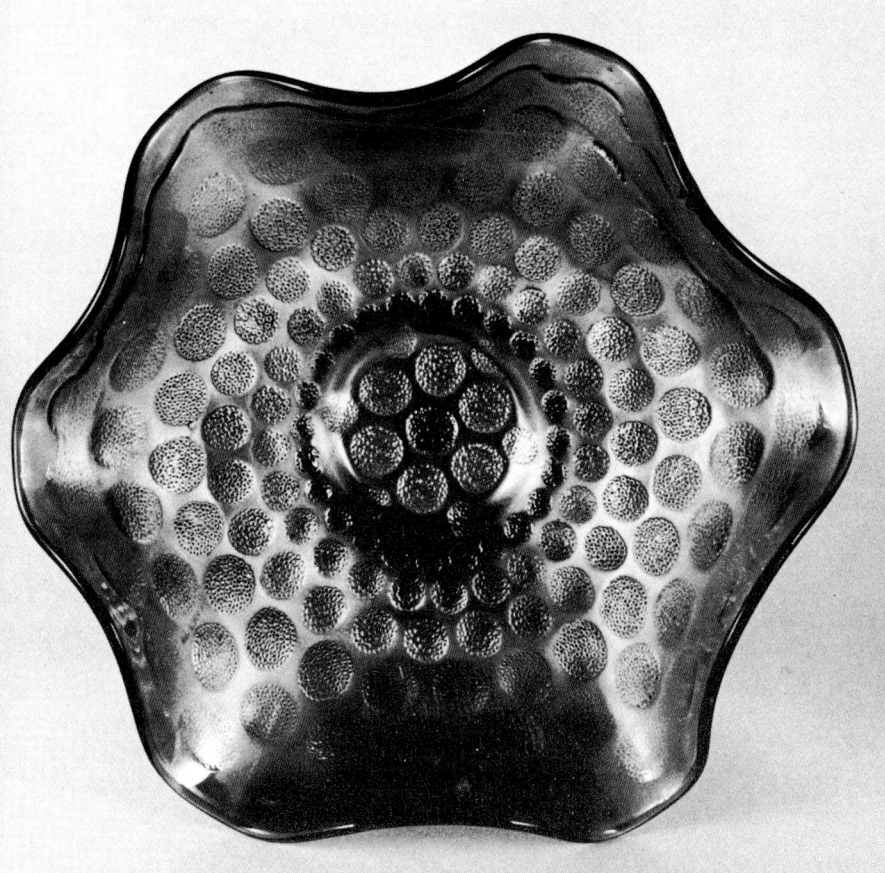

## BOWLS

**Grape and Cable** Diameter: 7½ inches. Base glass color: cobalt blue.
*(Fenton)* Base: smooth collar.

Four bunches of grapes, alternating with four large grape leaves, hang from vines entwined on a circular cable. Four small grape leaves decorate the center bottom to complete the interior pattern. The bowl has a smooth, iridized exterior. The typical Fenton rim, consisting of a wide scallop alternating with a small flute, should help you distinguish the Fenton Grape and Cable pattern from a similar one made by the Northwood Company, described below.

**Grape and Cable** Diameter: 8 inches. Base glass color: purple. Base:
*(Northwood)* smooth collar. Northwood mark.

Like the Fenton pattern described above (and pictured on the opposite page), this Northwood pattern also has four bunches of grapes alternating with four large grape leaves hung from vines, entwined on a circular cable. Here, too, there are four small leaves in the center of the bowl, and the exterior of the bowl is smooth and not iridized. (Northwood's Grape and Cable can also be found with their Basketweave pattern or their Plume and Snowflake pattern on the exterior. Tall, straight-sided pieces such as pitchers, tumblers, cookie jars, and hats have a Thumbprint pattern around the bottom.) This bowl has a ruffled, fluted rim and spectacular iridescence. Grape and Cable was an extremely popular pattern, and came in many different shapes and colors.

**Grape Leaves** Diameter: 8¾ inches. Base glass color: marigold on
**and Acorns** clear. Base: smooth collar.
*(Millersburg)*

Four large grape leaves alternate with acorns on the interior of this lovely bowl. There is one large grape leaf in the center. The exterior pattern is called Wide Panel and consists of twelve smooth, wide, iridized panels. The rim is scalloped. This pattern was also made by Fenton.

**Grape and Cable** *(Northwood)*      **Grape and Cable** *(Fenton)*

**Grape Leaves and Acorns** *(Millersburg)*      **Imperial's Grape** *(Imperial)*, page 45

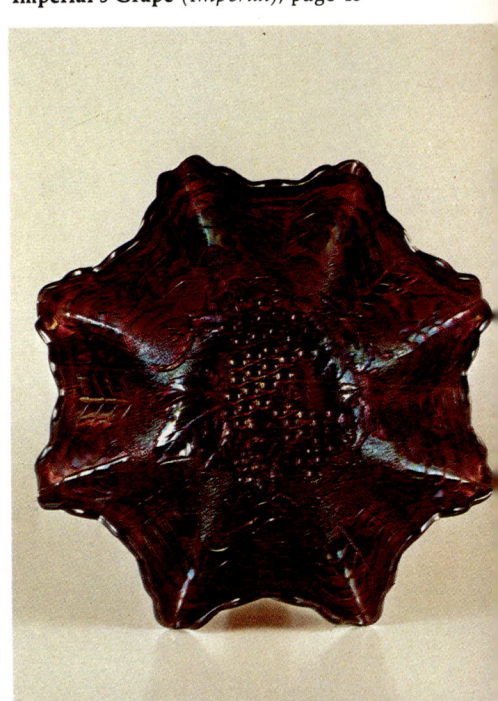

## BOWLS

**Imperial's Grape**
*(Imperial)*

Diameter: 11 inches. Base glass color: purple. Base: smooth collar. (See page 43.)

The interior pattern has large clusters of grapes on a leafy vine with two smaller clusters of grapes, all on a stippled background. The stippling ends in scallops halfway up the inside of the bowl. Four more smooth scallops continue to the top. The exterior features six large bunches of grapes on leafy vines placed on a stippled background, which is separated from the rim by a ridge of double scallops. This heavily raised design was one of the most popular grape patterns and was made in most shapes and colors. (Other examples are illustrated on pages 24 and 76.) Imperial's Grape has been reissued.

**Kookaburra Bird**
*Crystal Glass Ltd.,*
*Sydney, Australia)*

Diameter: 9½ inches. Base glass color: dark purple. Base: smooth collar.

This rare bowl gets its name from the Australian bird shown in the center. The bird is sitting on a branch surrounded by three large flowers and foliage. Above, two branches are tied together by a bow, and a butterfly hovers over the bird's head. Two large leaves attached to wild fern sprays are on the exterior. Iridized on both sides, this bowl has an extraordinarily dark color.

Originally thought to have been made in the United States and exported to Australia, further research has indicated that the bowl's origin is Australia. An application for registration of the Kookaburra pattern was made by Crystal Glass Ltd. in 1923. Bowls similar to this one, with the addition of the Australian registration number, have been found. Australian Carnival glass is most often seen in dark purple and marigold. The shapes found are compotes, bowls, and stemmed plates of various sizes.

---

Facing page: **Kookaburra Bird** *(Crystal Glass Ltd., Sydney, Australia)*

## 46 BOWLS

**Nippon**  
*(Northwood)*
Diameter: 8¾ inches. Base glass color: green. Base: smooth collar. Northwood mark.

Diameter: 8¾ inches. Base glass color: marigold on clear. Base: smooth collar.

The inside center of the Nippon bowl has a stylized flower in a raised, stippled circle surrounded by twelve draped panels. The exterior pattern is Basketweave.

**Open Rose**  
*(Imperial)*
Diameter: 7 inches. Base glass color: amber. Base: smooth collar. (See page 21.)

Two large, open roses on leafy stems and five buds on a stippled background ending in regular scallops are on the interior of this impressive bowl. Fine lines connect the scallops to the bowl's rim. The exterior pattern consists of three panels, each having one large, open rose and five rosebuds on a leafy stem. The wide panels are separated by three narrow panels with two daisy-like flowers on each, all on a stippled background. This very popular rose pattern was extensively produced in many shapes. Open Rose has been reissued by the Imperial Glass Company.

**Pansy**  
*(Imperial)*
Diameter: 8½ inches. Base glass color: purple. Base: twenty-four-point star.

The upper pattern shows four large, stemmed pansies and buds on a stippled background ending in a sawtooth edge. The exterior of this relish dish is the Quilted Diamonds pattern.

**Peach and Pear**
Diameter: 12½ inches. Base glass color: marigold on clear. Base: smooth collar. (See page 48.)

The interior of this oval banana bowl has a peach and a pear in the center surrounded by a wreath of leaves on a smooth background. Two pears at each end, and a peach with leaves and twigs, decorate the outside.

Two **Nippon** *(Northwood)* bowls, with the interior pattern displayed on the left and the exterior Basketweave pattern on the right

**Pansy** *(Imperial)*; **Poppy** *(Northwood)*, page 51

**Peacock and Grape** *(Fenton)*, page 51, showing the interior pattern

**Peacock and Grape** *(Fenton)*, page 51, exterior Bearded Berry pattern

**Peach and Pear,** page 46

**Star Medallion,** page 52

**Peacock Tail** *(Imperial),* page 51

Two **Vintage** bowls, page 52

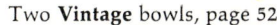

**Peacock and Grape** (Fenton)

Diameter: 9 inches. Base glass color: green. Base: smooth collar. (See page 48.)

A peacock alternates with a bunch of grapes on eight framed panels on the interior of this magnificent bowl. The center has a rosette of eight stylized peacock feathers on a smooth background. The exterior pattern, Bearded Berry, has three panels, each containing two bunches of berries.

**Peacock Tail** (Imperial)

Diameter: 8½ inches. Base glass color: marigold on clear. Base: smooth collar. (See page 49.)

Twelve panels of arcs radiate from a twelve-petaled center rosette and end in wide arcs on the interior of this fluted-rim bowl. The exterior pattern is Wide Panel.

**Persian Medallion** (Fenton)

Diameter: 8½ inches. Base glass color: green. Base: smooth collar. (See page 21.)

A border of irregularly shaped medallions with a large medallion in the center forms the famous Fenton Persian Medallion pattern. The bowl has an irregular ruffled, crimped edge with a smooth, iridized exterior. This spectacular design was used as a secondary pattern on many different Fenton shapes.

**Poppy** (Northwood)

Diameter: 8 inches. Base glass color: cobalt blue. Base: oval star. (See page 47.)

Four poppies on a stippled background are surrounded by feathery bands and enclosed by a string of beads. The bottom of this oval relish dish is ribbed.

**Smooth Rib**

Diameter: 7½ inches. Base glass color: clambroth. Base: twenty-four-point star. (See page 18.)

Fine raised ribs radiate from a smooth center, ending about one-quarter inch from the scalloped, fluted rim. The exterior is smooth and not iridized.

---

Facing page: **Stippled Ray** (Northwood), page 52

## 52 BOWLS

**Star Medallion**    Diameter: 6 inches. Base glass color: marigold on clear. Base: near-cut. (See page 49.)

Six star-cut medallions on a cane background are on the exterior of this near-cut pattern bowl. The interior is smooth and iridized.

**Stippled Flower**    Diameter: 8¼ inches. Base glass color: marigold on clear. Base: smooth collar. (See page 15.)

Smooth ribs radiate from behind a textured six-petaled flower in the center of this bowl. The exterior is smooth and opalescent.

**Stippled Ray**    Diameter: 11 inches. Base glass color: amethyst.
*(Northwood)*    Base: smooth collar. Northwood mark. (See page 50.)

Alternating smooth and stippled rays radiate from the raised circular center, which shows the embossed Northwood mark. The rim is deeply ruffled and fluted. The exterior is smooth and is not iridized.

**Vintage**    Diameter: 9 inches. Base glass color: green. Base: smooth collar. (See page 49.)

Diameter: 10 inches. Base glass color: marigold on clear. Base: thirty-point star. (See page 49.)

Another of the popular grape patterns, the green Vintage bowl has five clusters of grapes on a leafy vine. There is a large grape leaf in the center. The exterior pattern is Wide Panel. The ruffled-rim bowl has six clusters of grapes on leafy vines, with a large grape leaf in the center. The exterior pattern is Wide Panel.

**Whirling Leaves**    Diameter: 10 inches. Base glass color: marigold on
*(Millersburg)*    clear: Base: near-cut.

A pinwheel of four leaves with flowers between the leaves is on the interior of this Millersburg bowl. The Fine Cut in Ovals near-cut pattern is on the exterior.

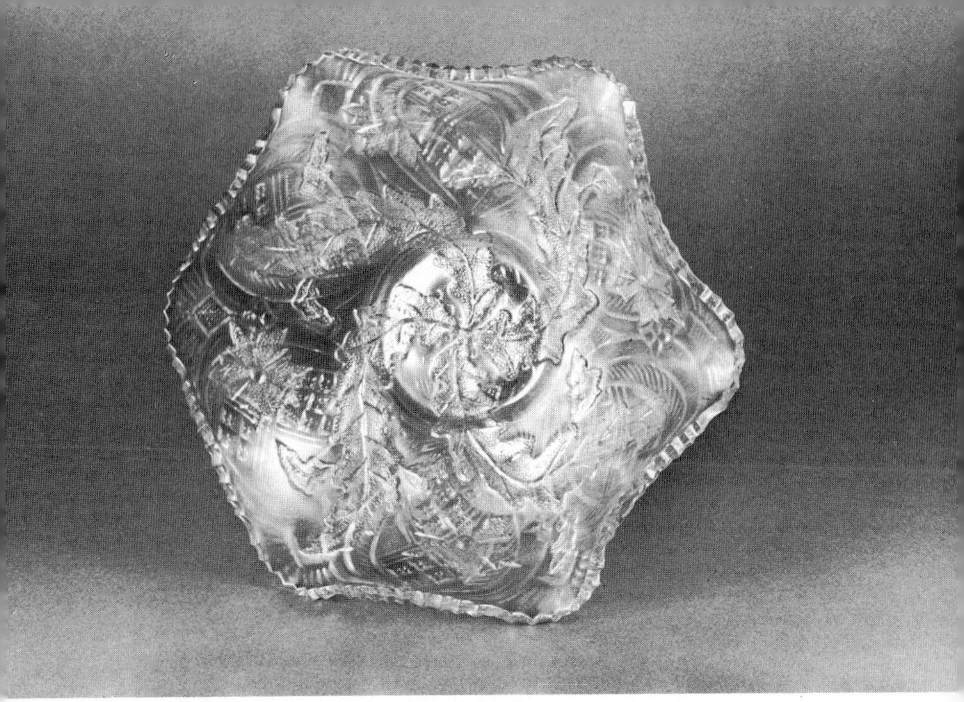

**Whirling Leaves** *(Millersburg)*, interior pattern

**Whirling Leaves** *(Millersburg)*, showing the Fine Cut in Ovals pattern on the exterior

# Bowls on Matching Stands

Punch bowls and some fruit bowls were made with separate matching stands. Punch bowl sets included six or twelve cups, and were made in many of the popular patterns and colors. The two-piece fruit bowls are an uncommon shape, and were made in very few patterns.

**Orange Tree** *(Fenton)* — Height: 9 inches. Diameter: 11 inches. Cup height: 2½ inches. Base glass color: marigold on clear. Base: matching stand. (See page 11.)

The exterior of this magnificent punch bowl, with its matching stand and cup hooks, has six large orange trees on a smooth background with a narrow, patterned border. Different motifs were used in this border over the life of the pattern. The matching cups have five orange trees on the outside. The cups and the bowl and stand are unpatterned and iridized on the interior. Orange Tree was an extremely popular pattern and was made in many other shapes and colors, sometimes combined with other patterns.

**Twins** *(Imperial)* — Height: 9 inches. Diameter: 9½ inches. Base glass color: marigold on clear. Base: matching stand.

The interior of this two-piece fruit bowl on a separate stand is smooth and iridized. The exterior of the bowl and the stand are in the near-cut pattern Twins. The stand is the same type as those made for punch bowls.

---

Facing page: **Twins** *(Imperial)*. This impressive pattern is one of the intricately designed near-cut motifs.

# Footed Bowls

Footed bowls were made in a wide variety of sizes. The largest deep, round shapes were used for oranges. Large oval shapes held bananas, and a variety of smaller sizes were made for nuts and candies.

**Butterfly and Berry** *(Fenton)*
Diameter: 5 inches. Base glass color: cobalt blue. Base: four ball-and-claw feet. (See page 59.)
The interior of this berry bowl shows a butterfly surrounded by a wreath of leaves and berries, on a smooth background. The exterior of the bowl has twelve panels of alternating butterflies and berries.

**Double Dutch**
Diameter: 8½ inches. Base glass color: marigold on clear. Base: three feet. (See page 60.)
A man is fishing in a boat on the interior of this bowl. Behind him is a Dutch landscape with windmills. Under the rim of the bowl is a floral band. The exterior is smooth and iridized.

**Leaf and Beads** *(Northwood)*
Diameter: 7½ inches. Base glass color: marigold on clear. Base: three treebark-textured feet.
Vertical stippled leaves rise three-quarters of the way up the exterior of this footed bowl. At the apex of each leaf a string of beads extends to the scalloped rim. The background is smooth. The interior of the bowl has a smooth center from which twenty-three petals radiate halfway up the sides. Smooth ribs are behind the petals. Variations of the Leaf and Beads bowl are sometimes iridized on only one side. Other shapes do not have the many-petaled flower in the center of the ribbing. Although the Northwood mark does not appear on this particular piece, it has been attributed to Northwood.

---

Facing page: **Leaf and Beads** *(Northwood)*, one of Northwood's many naturalistic patterns

## FOOTED BOWLS

**Lustre Rose**
*(Imperial)*

Diameter: 11½ inches. Base glass color: clambroth. Base: collar with centered rose on three scroll feet.

The interior pattern on this large, deep bowl consists of four large open roses on stems, with leaves and six buds, on a stippled background bordered by a triple sawtooth design. The exterior pattern, a variation of the interior pattern, has three panels, each with three stemmed, open roses with a leaf and a bud, on a stippled background separated by double-draped panels extending from the feet to three thin, twisted vines that circle the outside of the bowl.

**Panther**
*(Fenton)*

Diameter: 5 inches. Base glass color: marigold on clear. Base: four ball-and-claw feet.

A large, leafy branch divides the interior of this berry bowl. There are two crouching panthers and foliage, one on each side of the branch. The Butterfly and Berry pattern is on the exterior.

**Peacock at the Fountain**
*(Northwood)*

Height: 6 inches. Diameter: 10 inches. Base glass color: marigold on clear. Base: three scroll feet. Northwood mark. (See page 60.)

Three panels, each containing a stylized peacock and a fountain, circle the exterior of this footed orange bowl. (Sometimes this pattern has a bumblebee above the peacock's head.) The panels are surrounded by a large, beaded border, top and bottom. The Northwood mark is on the smooth, iridized interior. Peacock at the Fountain was a very popular pattern with well-executed details, and it was made in many other shapes and colors.

**Stag and Holly**
*(Fenton)*

Diameter: 10 inches. Base glass color: marigold on clear. Base: three scroll feet. (See page 60.)

A large multi-petaled flower is in the center of this animal pattern bowl. Standing on the flower are four stags, separated by large, leafy plants with berries. Wide Panel is the pattern on the exterior.

**Panther** *(Fenton)*; **Butterfly and Berry** *(Fenton)*, page 57

**Lustre Rose** *(Imperial)*

**Double Dutch,** page 57

**Stag and Holly** *(Fenton),* page 58

**Peacock at the Fountain** *(Northwood),* page 58

**Thistle** *(Fenton)*, page 62, showing the exterior Waterlily and Cattails pattern

**Thistle** *(Fenton)*, page 62, interior pattern

## FOOTED BOWLS

**Thistle**
*(Fenton)*

Length: 10½ inches. Base glass color: amethyst. Base: four scroll feet. (See pages 22 and 61.)

The interior pattern of this oval banana bowl has four stylized thistles bordered by a geometric-patterned band. Waterlily and Cattails is the exterior pattern. Four cattail plants alternate with four large waterlilies. The four large scroll feet make this a very sturdy piece.

**Three Fruits**
*(Northwood)*

Diameter: 9 inches. Base glass color: fiery amethyst. Base: three spatulate feet. (See page 6.)

The well-known Three Fruits pattern appears on the interior of this footed fruit bowl. It consists of a wreath of apples, pears, and cherries with three small leaves in the center, on a smooth, iridized background. Another version of this pattern has three cherries in the center of the wreath instead of three leaves. Whether or not the Northwood trademark appears, this pattern has been definitely identified as belonging to the Northwood Company. The exterior pattern, Plume and Snowflake, has three snowflakes alternating with three plumes. The bowl was also made with a smooth or Basketweave exterior, and in other colors.

**Wild Rose**
*(Northwood)*

Diameter: 7 inches. Base glass color: green. Base: three small scroll feet. Northwood mark.

Each foot on the outside of the bowl is surrounded by a large, fan-shaped shell. An open rose in the center of two leaves on a stippled background alternates with the shell. The interior of this bowl is smooth and iridized, but the Wild Rose pattern is also made with a Fine Rib interior. An unusual feature of this piece is the open, heart-shaped border.

---

Facing page: **Wild Rose** *(Northwood)*. This footed bowl has a unique open-worked border of hearts.

**Smooth**

**Vintage; Scotch Thistle; Stippled Ray**

# Compotes

The open compote is a deep bowl shape on a stemmed, flat or slightly domed, footed base. The sizes most commonly found are about five to six inches high. They were made in many patterns and colors, and were both useful and decorative. Usually, the pattern is found on the interior, and the exterior is smooth.

Larger compotes (nine to ten inches high) were made in smaller quantities and are hard to find. These larger pieces tend to be more elaborate in design, some with patterns on both the interior and exterior. Compotes were also made with matching covers, but very few patterns are known in this style and these pieces are quite rare.

**Scotch Thistle**  Height: 5½ inches. Diameter: 6 inches. Base glass color: green. Base: stemmed foot.

Three Scotch thistles are surrounded by textured swags on this footed compote. There is no pattern on the beautifully iridized exterior.

**Smooth**  Height: 5½ inches. Diameter: 6 inches. Base glass color: marigold on clear. Base: stemmed foot.

The interior of this unpatterned piece has a delicate pink and gold iridescence. The exterior is not iridized.

**Stippled Ray**  Height: 4½ inches. Diameter: 6 inches. Base glass color: green. Base: stemmed foot.

Alternating smooth and stippled rays radiate from the center of the interior of this compote. The smooth exterior is iridized.

**Vintage**  Height: 6 inches. Diameter: 6 inches. Base glass color: green. Base: stemmed foot.

Five bunches of grapes are on a smooth background inside the bowl of this compote. The iridized exterior is unpatterned.

# Rosebowls

Small and round, rosebowls have a characteristic upper edge which is turned in toward the center, either evenly or in deep folds. Rosebowls were made with low collar bases and in a variety of footed designs. Some of the more unusual footed pieces were made in a goblet shape with a stemmed, broad-footed base. Most rosebowls are patterned on the exterior and have a smooth interior. However, some were made with secondary interior patterns. Rosebowls are found in every Carnival glass color but not in a wide range of patterns, although some patterns were made especially for them.

**Daisy and Plume** *(Northwood)* — Height: 5 inches. Base glass color: fiery amethyst. Base: three feet. Northwood mark.

Three large daisies on a stippled background alternate with two plumes that rise from the feet. The Raspberry pattern is on the inside of this lovely bowl.

**Grape Delight** — Height: 4 inches. Base glass color: white. Base: six feet. (See page 12.)

Three bunches of grapes on vines alternate with a large grape leaf on the outside of the rosebowl. The interior is smooth and iridized.

---

Facing page: **Daisy and Plume** *(Northwood)*. This stately rosebowl displays the deep lustre and satin sheen found on many of the Northwood products.

# Nappies

Nappies are small flat bowls with one handle. They are round or triangular, or any variation of these shapes. The sides of a nappy are high enough to hold a small quantity of jam, pickles, or other condiments.

**Leaf Rays**

Length: 7 inches from handle to tip. Base glass color: white. Base: smooth collar.

Length: 6 inches from handle to tip. Base glass color: marigold on amethyst. Base: smooth collar.

A ten-petaled flower is in the center of each of these heart-shaped nappies. Ten large stippled leaves extend up the sides. The exterior is smooth and not iridized. The shape of the slightly larger Leaf Rays nappy is triangular, but the two are otherwise similar in all respects.

**Pansy**
*(Imperial)*

Diameter: 5 inches. Base glass color: marigold on clear. Base: twenty-four-point star.

On the inside of this nappy are four large, stemmed, open pansies and several buds on a stippled background, surrounded by a sawtooth edge. The exterior pattern, Quilted Diamonds, is composed of alternating smooth and stippled diamond shapes with a bead at each intersection. The outer rim is also beaded. The handle resembles a textured twig. Pansy is one of the popular flower patterns and was also made in many other shapes, such as bowls, pitchers, and tumblers.

Two **Leaf Rays** nappies

**Pansy** *(Imperial)*, showing the Quilted Diamonds pattern on the exterior

**Fruits and Flowers** *(Northwood)*  **Question Marks**

**Star and File**

# Bonbons

Bonbons are two-handled bowls which are either stemmed or flat. The flat shape has a shallow bowl with two opposite sides turned up where the handles are attached. In the stemmed version the bowl is usually deeper, but the double handles are attached in the same manner. The stems are footed and quite low.

Bonbons were made in great quantities for holding candies or calling cards. They were often made in fruit and flower or near-cut patterns.

**Fruits and Flowers (Northwood)**

Height: 4 inches. Base glass color: cobalt blue. Base: stemmed foot. Northwood mark.

The difference between the Fruits and Flowers pattern and the Three Fruits pattern of Northwood is the addition of small, three-petaled flowers. The Northwood mark is in the center of the bowl. The outer pattern is Basketweave. Fenton has reissued a version of Fruits and Flowers, but it is not made from the original molds.

**Question Marks**

Height: 3¾ inches. Base glass color: marigold on clear. Base: stemmed foot.

There are eight beaded question marks alternating with eight three-petaled florets on a smooth, iridized background in the interior of this bonbon. The handles and footed stem are clear. The exterior is smooth and not iridized.

**Star and File**

Height: 6½ inches. Base glass color: marigold on clear. Base: near-cut.

The near-cut pattern Star and File is on the exterior of this two-handled bonbon. The interior is smooth and iridized.

# Table Sets

Table sets included creamers, covered butter dishes, covered sugar bowls, and spooners, or spoon holders. These sets often came in patterns that matched the water sets. (Water sets are discussed on page 74.) A milk pitcher was often used with the table sets. Smaller than the large water pitcher, the milk pitcher was of medium size and made only in the most popular patterns. Two-piece breakfast sets—a creamer and sugar—were also made. Individual creamer-shaped pieces were used as sauce boats.

**Curved Star**  Height: 5 inches. Base glass color: marigold on clear. Base: twenty-point star.

Curved Star, a near-cut pattern, is used on the exterior of this cream pitcher.

**Fashion**  
*(Imperial)*  Height: 3¼ inches. Base glass color: marigold on clear. Base: near-cut. (This pattern is illustrated in color on page 21.)

The popular near-cut pattern Fashion is on the exterior of this creamer and sugar. Fashion was made in a multitude of shapes and colors.

**Lea**  Height: 3½ inches. Base glass color: marigold on clear. Base: three feet.

Three stylized hearts are on the stippled interior base of this creamer. The inner sides are smooth panels. Six stippled panels banded with ribbing are on the exterior.

**Pineapple**  Height: 4½ inches. Base glass color: marigold on clear. Base: pinwheel.

Three inverted pineapples on a diamond-point background are on the outside of this small cream pitcher.

**Fashion** *(Imperial)*

**Curved Star; Pineapple; Lea**

**Star Medallion**   Height: 6 inches. Base glass color: marigold on clear. Base: cut-star.

A near-cut pattern which consists of star-cut medallions on a cane background is on the exterior of this milk pitcher. Many other shapes were made in this popular pattern.

**Thistle and Thorn**   Height: 4 inches. Base glass color: marigold on clear. Base: four twig feet.

Small thistles and flowers protrude from a large leaf on the exterior of this round cream pitcher. The handle and four feet are twig-textured. Two small branches extend around the top and meet at the spout.

## Water Sets

One of the most popular household items made in Carnival glass was the water set, consisting of a large pitcher with six matching tumblers. The most commonly found pitcher shape was the enlarged mug made in many patterns. Second in popularity was the tankard. There was also a globular or bulbous pitcher often found with a ruffled rim. The footed and dome-footed style pitchers often had footed tumblers to match. Because of their more decorative shape, the bulbous and footed pitchers were easily broken and are now difficult to find. Carafes, or water bottles, were also made for table use.

**Floral and Grape**
*(Fenton)*   Pitcher height: 8½ inches. Tumbler height: 4¼ inches. Base glass color: amethyst. Base: smooth.

Another popular grape pattern, the Floral and Grape combines bunches of grapes with daisies. The pitcher is bulbous, with a ruffled top and applied handle. There are six matching tumblers. This water set was presented to the owners of the Wheatland Hotel in Lancaster, Pennsylvania, as a grand opening gift.

**Thistle and Thorn; Lustre Rose** *(Imperial)*, page 77; **Star Medallion**

**Floral and Grape** *(Fenton)*

**Imperial's Grape** (*Imperial*)

**Painted Cherries**, page 78; **Diamond** (*Millersburg*); **Stork and Rushes**, page 78

**Imperial's Grape**
*(Imperial)*

Height: 8½ inches. Base glass color: amethyst. Base: smooth.

This handsome pair of water bottles has heavily raised bunches of grapes on a stippled background swirled around the exterior. The Imperial's Grape water bottle has a narrow neck with a slightly flaring rim. The owner's great aunt recevied these bottles as premiums from a tea company for saving coupons.

**Lustre Rose**
*(Imperial)*

Height: 8½ inches. Base glass color: amber. Base: twenty-four-point star. (See page 75.)

There are two large, open roses with buds on a stippled background on the exterior of this pitcher. The interior of the pitcher is Smooth Rib. The handle is ribbed also.

# Tumblers

Carnival glass tumblers were part of the popular water sets which consisted of a pitcher and matching drinking glasses. Collectors often specialize in tumblers since it is difficult and costly to collect complete matching sets.

**Diamond**
*(Millersburg)*

Height: 4 inches. Base glass color: green. Base: smooth.

Nine diamonds circle this tumbler. The interior is smooth and iridized.

**Oriental Poppy**
*(Northwood)*

Height: 4½ inches. Base glass color: amethyst. Base: twenty-four-point star. Northwood mark. (Page 79.)

A poppy with two buds on a leafy stem is heavily raised on the exterior panels of the tumbler. The Northwood mark appears in the smooth, iridized interior. Oriental Poppy is a popular pattern and can be found in many other colors and shapes.

**Painted Cherries**   Height: 3⅝ inches. Base glass color: cobalt blue. Base: smooth. (See page 76.)
Three painted cherries are on a smooth, iridized background. The smooth interior is also iridized.

**Raspberry**   Height: 4½ inches. Base glass color: green. Base:
*(Northwood)*   smooth. Northwood mark.
The outer bottom of this tumbler has a Basketweave pattern. Above the Basketweave border are three bunches of raspberries with leaves and flowers. The interior of the tumbler is ribbed.

**Singing Birds**   Height: 4 inches. Base glass color: green. Base: twenty-
*(Northwood)*   four-point star. Northwood mark.
On each side of the tumbler's outer surface are two birds back to back on a branch with leaves and flowers. The background has eight panels. The smooth, iridized interior has the Northwood mark.

**Stork and Rushes**   Height: 3⅞ inches. Base glass color: cobalt blue. Base: smooth. (See page 76.)
Two storks among rushes are facing each other on two sides of the tumbler. A row of beads is placed above and below the storks. The interior is smooth and iridized.

# *Bottles*

Carnival glass bottles were made for soda, whiskey, and wine companies as containers for their products. On rare occasions bottles are found with the original paper labels intact, which adds to their value.

**Canada Dry**   Height: 9¾ inches. Base glass color: clear. Capacity: two pints.
Height: 9¾ inches. Base glass color: marigold on clear. Capacity: two pints.

**Raspberry** (Northwood); **Singing Birds** (Northwood); **Oriental Poppy** (Northwood), page 77

**Canada Dry; Continental Distilling Corporation,** page 81; **Canada Dry**

The letters "Canada Dry" are embossed on each side of the neck of the clear bottle. The smooth base has a triangle with a C in the center and a smaller triangle above it. An embossed circle around the base of the stippled marigold bottle reads "Canada Dry Incorporated." Within this circle are the letters "Ginger Ale 2 D."

**Continental Distilling Corporation**

Height: 9½ inches. Base glass color: marigold on clear. Capacity: one quart. (See page 79.)

This whiskey bottle has an allover waffle pattern. A large, smooth diamond is indented on the back where a label was affixed. The front has an indented, smooth circle with a raised coat of arms. At the bottom there is a horizontal smooth, indented panel with raised lettering reading "Continental Distilling Corporation, Philadelphia, Pa." The base of the bottle reads "Patent No. 90133," embossed over an inverted triangle. The Continental bottle was also made with a smooth surface, and in a seven-inch pint size.

**Golden Wedding**

Height: 4 inches. Base glass color: light marigold on clear. Capacity: 1/10 pint.

Height: 7¾ inches. Base glass color: marigold on clear. Capacity: one pint.

The front of the Golden Wedding whiskey bottle has a smooth rectangular panel where a paper label was affixed. The back of the bottle has a smaller smooth rectangular panel with a large bell embossed above it. The background has an overall pinstripe pattern with garlands of bells framing the panels on each side. The miniature bottle still has its original paper labels and tax stamp on it. Golden Wedding whiskey was a product of Jos. S. Finch and Co., Schenley, Pa.

---

Facing page: Two **Golden Wedding** bottles

## Plates

Carnival glass plates were primarily decorative pieces, and it was popular to hang them on the wall as decor. It is sometimes difficult to distinguish between a shallow bowl and a plate; plates should measure no more than one to one-and-a-half inches high. Plates usually have smooth rims, although scalloped rims are occasionally found. There are a few footed pieces, but most plates have a collar base.

Although plates are generally harder to find than other shapes, they were made in many of the popular Carnival glass patterns.

**Four Flowers**  Diameter: 6½ inches. Base glass color: marigold on clear. Base: smooth collar. (See page 15.)

The interior pattern of the plate has four flowers, whose stems are crossed in the center, alternating with arcs. The opalescent back is smooth.

**Ship and Stars**  Diameter: 8 inches. Base glass color: marigold on clear. Base: smooth collar.

The exterior pattern of a three-masted sailing ship on tiny waves is in the center of the plate. Stippled on the border are tiny stars and raised veins. The interior is smooth and iridized.

---

Facing page: **Ship and Stars.** This plate combines a scenic motif with an ornamental border.

# Baskets

Baskets were considered purely decorative pieces. Most have one or two handles and were used to hold candies or short-stemmed flowers. Often they were placed on a shelf or a mantel to provide a touch of color.

**Beaded Basket**  Height: 5 inches. Diameter 5½ inches. Base glass color: marigold on clear. Base: smooth.

Two diagonal basketweave patterns are separated by a horizontal weave. Topping each of the three bands of weaving is a row of beads. Arched panels form the rim. There are two clear handles. The interior is smooth and iridized.

**Fenton's Basket**  Diameter: 5½ inches. Base glass color: marigold on clear. Base: smooth collar.
*(Fenton)*

Diameter: 5½ inches. Base glass color: cobalt blue. Base: smooth collar.

On the cobalt basket, the exterior basketweave pattern has two rows of openwork at the top. There is a lovely silver iridescence inside. The marigold basket is another version of Fenton's Basket.

**Venetian Thread**  Diameter: 5¾ inches. Height: 6 inches. Base glass color: marigold on clear. Base: smooth.

This delicate basket appears to sit on double bands. It has twisted, clear-glass handles which have been applied separately and attached to each side by a beaded button. The interior and exterior are iridized. The ruffled rim ends in six cobalt-blue stripes.

**Beaded Basket**  **Venetian Thread**

Two examples of **Fenton's Basket** *(Fenton)*

**Lustre Flute** *(Northwood)*; **Grape and Cable** *(Northwood)*; **Grape Arbor** *(Northwood)*

A pair of **Wide Panel** candlesticks, page 88

## Hats

Hats resemble baskets without the handles. They were primarily decorative but they may have been used to hold candy, nuts, toothpicks, or wooden matches.

**Grape and Cable**
*(Northwood)*

Height: 3 inches. Diameter: 6 inches. Base glass color: marigold on clear. Base: smooth collar. Northwood mark.

Four bunches of grapes alternating with four large grape leaves hang from vines which are entwined on a circular cable. Around the bottom of the hat is the Northwood Thumbprint pattern. The interior is smooth and iridized, with a raised Northwood mark. The top rim is flaring and scalloped. The Grape and Cable pattern combined with the Thumbprint indicates a Northwood piece even if a mark is not present.

**Grape Arbor**
*(Northwood)*

Height: 3½ inches. Diameter: 5½ inches. Base glass color: white. Base: smooth collar. Northwood mark.

Three bunches of grapes alternate with three large grape leaves on an arbor on the exterior pattern of this hat. The interior is smooth and iridized.

**Lustre Flute**
*(Northwood)*

Height: 3½ inches. Diameter: 4 inches. Base glass color: marigold on clear. Base: twenty-two-point star. Northwood mark.

The exterior pattern of this hat is one of concave ribs bordered by a band of diamond points. The interior is smooth and iridized.

## Candlesticks

Glass candlesticks became popular with the invention of pressed glass. They had simple forms, and a touch of color provided elegance. Not too many patterns are known to have been used for Carnival glass candlesticks. They were often sold as part of a set which included a matching console bowl.

**Crackle**  Height: 7 inches. Base glass color: marigold on clear. Base: hollow.

The pattern on this pair of candlesticks consists of six panels with very fine raised veins on a stippled background. This pattern, called Tree of Life in earlier, non-iridized pressed pattern glass, was an attempt to reproduce an effect known as Venetian Frosted glass or Craquelle.

**Soda Gold**  Height: 3½ inches. Base glass color: marigold on clear. Base: domed.

Soda Gold, like Crackle, is another version of the pressed glass Tree of Life pattern. Soda Gold is a heavily veined pattern on a background of tiny linear dots, while Crackle has fine veins on a stippled background.

**Wide Panel**  Height: 6½ inches. Base glass color: marigold on clear. Base: hollow. (See page 86.)

The pattern on this pair of smooth, iridized candlesticks has six panels that end in arcs, both top and bottom.

---

Facing page: A pair of **Crackle** candlesticks and, in the center, a single **Soda Gold** candleholder

# Hatpins

Hatpins are among the hard-to-find items of Carnival glass. When purchasing a hatpin, check to see that the pin is secured in a sleevelike flange that is part of the mold. This assures you that the piece was originally made as a hatpin and is not a converted button.

All the hatpins shown are between one and one-and-a-half inches in diameter. The base glass color is dark purple. (The glass on the underside of these pins appears to be black; however, when they are held up to direct sunlight, a deep purple shows through.) Hatpins can also be found in marigold.

| | |
|---|---|
| Basketweave Variant | A center of two different Basketweave patterns is surrounded by a gold circle on a faceted rim. |
| Bumblebees | Three bumblebees form a triangle, with a small raised bead in the center. |
| Butterfly | This oval hatpin has a large, winged butterfly and a bead at each end. This pattern has also been called Scarab. |
| Cattails | Six cattails are surrounded by swirling lines in this Art Nouveau-inspired design. |
| Pinwheel | Two intersecting squares with pinwheel lines radiate from the center on a background of tiny beads. This hatpin has an unusually heavy bronze iridescence. |
| Top o' the Morning | This stylized rooster has tail feathers that swirl around the rim of the hatpin. |
| Veiling | Raised vertical and horizontal lines cross on a finely veiled background. One raised bead is in the center of the pin, surrounded by four others, all of which are placed on the intersections of the lines. |

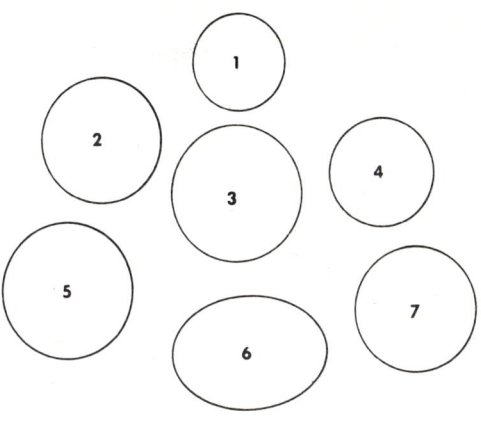

1. Veiling
2. Basketweave Variant
3. Bumblebees
4. Pinwheel
5. Cattails
6. Butterfly
7. Top o' the Morning

**Covered Hen**  **Handbag**

**Mayflower** *(Imperial)* lampshade, page 94

## *Miscellaneous*

**Carnival Holly** — Height: 4½ inches. Diameter: 4 inches. Base glass color: cobalt blue. Base: stemmed foot. (See page 95.)

The interior of this sherbet shows five sprigs of holly and berries with groups of three berries radiating from the center of the cup on a background of stippled rays. Only the upper part of the exterior is iridized. Considered a Christmas pattern, Carnival Holly is frequently found on bowls and other shapes.

**Covered Hen** — Dish length: 8 inches; width: 5¾ inches. Hen length: 6⅞ inches; width: 4⅜ inches. Base glass color: cobalt blue. Base: waffle pattern, with a small, raised oval.

This covered oval dish of a hen and chicks, used for holding mustard, is in two pieces, both of them iridized inside and out. The sides of the lower piece have twenty-four concave panels, and there is stippling under the rim. The lid has a hen sitting on a nest. On each side of the hen are three chicks.

**Frog** — Diameter: 2¼ inches. Base glass color: marigold on clear. Base: flat, smooth. (See page 95.)

Frogs were used in bowls for holding flower arrangements.

**Grape and Cable (Northwood)** — Height: 3 inches. Base glass color: amethyst. Base: flat, smooth. Northwood mark. (See page 95.)

Bunches of grapes alternating with large grape leaves hang from a cable which encircles this punch cup. The interior is smooth and iridized.

**Handbag** — Handle width: 5 inches. Color of beads: blue and purple.

Rows of tiny blue and purple iridescent beads form vertical stripes that narrow as they reach the top. The handbag frame is of Dutch silver.

**Mayflower**
*(Imperial)*

Height: 3¾ inches. Base glass color: marigold on clear. (See page 92.)

The outer surface of this lovely lampshade has a large, stylized flower alternating with a bunch of leaves tied by a ribbon, on a stippled background. Both the interior and exterior are iridized. The Mayflower pattern was made in other shapes as well.

**Orange Tree**
*(Fenton)*

Height: 3½ inches. Base glass color: cobalt blue. Base: flat, smooth.

Six orange trees encircle this handled mug. They are bordered above and below by the Fenton Fish Scale band. The interior is smooth and iridized.

## *Insulators*

Insulators were first made in the early 1840s to fit over wooden pegs on telegraph poles. The groove in the glass was used for tying the wires. It was difficult to keep insulators on the pegs, so in 1865 Louis Cauvet invented an insulator with interior threads to match the threads on the pegs. In the 1870s there was a great demand for insulators for telephone and electric lines. Insulators without interior threads are much harder to find and much more valuable than the threaded ones.

**Bugeye**
*(Hemingray*
*Glass Company)*

Height 3⅞ inches. Base glass color: marigold on clear.
The words "Hemingray No. D512" appear on this threaded insulator.

**Corning**
**Number 63**
*(Corning Glass Co.)*

Height: 3¼ inches. Base glass color: marigold on clear.
This threaded Carnival glass insulator reads "Made in U.S.A."

**Orange Tree** *(Fenton)*; **Carnival Holly,** page 93; **Grape and Cable,** *(Northwood),* page 93

**Corning Number 63** insulator *(Corning Glass Company)*; **Frog,** page 93; **Bugeye** insulator *(Hemingray Glass Company)*

# Later Iridized Glass

Carnival glass was produced between 1905 and 1925, and any iridized glass made after that is usually called late Carnival glass. However, much of the iridescent, machine-made glassware that appeared between the 1920s and the 1940s is known as Depression glass.

Depression glass was a machine-made, useful, and decorative glassware. It was produced in clear glass as well as in a variety of colors and was sometimes iridized. It was dinnerware and giftware made totally by machine, cheaply mass-produced, and nationally distributed. It was made of the same glass that was used for commercial bottles and jars—a much poorer quality of glass than that which had been used for Carnival glass.

Using glass for dishware and cook-and-serve items was a novelty in the 1920s. For the first time in history, colored glass dinner sets for everyday use were inexpensive. Even earthenware could not compete in price with Depression glass. Because it was so inexpensive, it was used as premiums and giveaways. Individual pieces or entire sets of dishes were given away at the movies, with a set of furniture, or in return for saving a particular company's coupons.

There was no handwork or hand-decorating involved in the manufacture of Depression glass, as there was with some of the Carnival glass pieces. The glass was completely machine-molded and its manufacture

---

Facing page: A perfume bottle, a Texas hat, and a Bambi powder jar—three iridized Depression glass giftware designs

was entirely automated. The designs were etched or cut into the molds. Some of the Depression glass patterns were based on traditional designs. Others used the so-called modern geometric Art Deco style. Often flawed and poorly finished, busy patterns and bright colors helped disguise the poor workmanship. Since Depression glass was intended for everyday use, the patterns were placed on the exterior or underside to avoid damage from flatware—and so food particles wouldn't get caught in the indentations of the designs.

Because Depression glass had to be produced as economically as possible, only colors that were inexpensive to create were used. Green and yellow (obtained from iron), blue (from chromium or copper), and pink (from selenium) were the colors made in the greatest quantities. Few patterns are available in red and purple because these colors were far more expensive to produce, and they are usually among the rarities.

Not many of the companies which produced Depression glass featured iridescence on their tableware. When they did, it was usually a cheap process that did not involve refiring the pieces after the iridescence had been applied. Often these iridescent finishes were just sprayed on after the glassware had been made. Special names were used to distinguish this type of finish. Golden Glow, Sunburst, and Rose Glow were used by the Federal Glass Company. The Dunbar Glass Company had an iridescent orange-pink color called Peach Lustre, used on beverage sets.

## THE FEDERAL GLASS COMPANY

A major manufacturer of Depression glass, the Federal Glass Company of Columbus, Ohio, made Carnival-colored glass. A well-known pattern that came with an iridescent finish was Normandie, also called Bouquet and Lattice, because the design consisted of bouquets of flowers alternating with latticelike motifs. This pattern is popular with Carnival glass collectors. Nor-

LATER IRIDIZED GLASS 99

mandie was made in complete dinner sets with matching serving pieces. The colors were pink, amber, green, and crystal-clear, as well as the iridescent finish called Sunburst, which came in two shades: Golden Glow, an iridescent orange, and Rose Glow, and iridescent pink.

Madrid, one of Federal's most famous patterns, was made from 1932 to 1938. This mold-etched design

---

This Normandie pattern (also known as Bouquet and Lattice) was made by the Federal Glass Company. It came in two shades of an iridescent finish called Sunburst.

came in a flashed-on iridescent finish as well as in green, pink, blue, amber, and crystal-clear. The most often seen shapes with the Carnival finish were a console bowl and matching candlesticks.

## THE JEANNETTE GLASS COMPANY

Another large company that iridized glassware was the Jeannette Glass Company of Jeannette, Pennsylvania. One of their patterns, Iris and Herringbone, first appeared between 1928 and 1932 in crystal-clear. Occasionally, pieces were made in pink and green. A later iridized reissue of this pattern was produced in 1969. Its design of large irises and leaves on a fine herringbone background derives from Art Nouveau.

Three other late patterns were iridized by Jeannette. Louisa, which dates from the 1950s, was made in a

A popular Depression glass pattern iridized by the Jeannette Glass Company in the 1960s: Iris and Herringbone

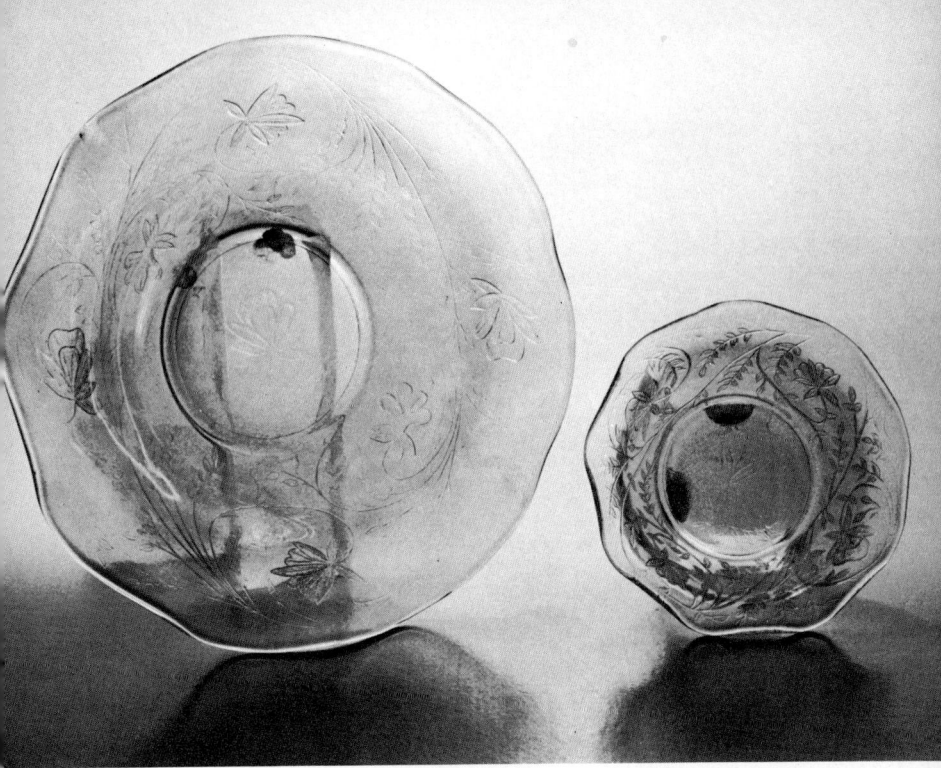

Louisa, a 1950s pattern made by Jeannette, has a sprayed-on iridescent finish called Floragold.

sprayed-on iridescent finish called Floragold. The pattern is composed of delicate sprays of raised leaves and flowers. Pieces of Louisa are being collected by Depression glass enthusiasts even though it is a product of the 1950s.

Anniversary, first produced between 1947 and 1949 in pink, was reissued in the 1970s in crystal-clear and iridescent. Holiday, or Button and Bows, also dates from 1947-1949, and was first made in pink and later iridized.

## GIFTWARE

Giftware in glass was extremely popular during the Depression years. These glass items had the virtue of looking expensive but not costing much. An enormous

amount of mass-produced giftware was made in a variety of styles. Many of them were given as premiums, and many were specially packaged for giving. Some were even used as prizes at carnivals. Among the many giftware items were cigarette boxes, ashtrays, perfume bottles, powder jars, relish dishes, cake plates, barware, beverage sets, cookie jars, banks, and kitchen ware. Many of the pieces were given an iridized finish to make them even more attractive.

Among the giftware items made by the Jeannette Glass Company during the Depression were a series of powder jars decorated with figurines on the lid. Either a cat, rabbit, donkey, scottie, French poodle, or deer, later called Bambi, was featured. These powder jars came in crystal-clear or pink as well as an iridized marigold.

Later, the Anchor Hocking Company of Lancaster, Ohio, produced a number of iridized glass banks. Some were made in an iridized marigold. Among the more popular banks were the Liberty Bell, the large and small Pig banks, a Globe or World bank, and a Barrel bank made in 1949; the Wise Owl made in 1952; and the Eagle and Star, shaped like a decanter, made in 1966.

---

Facing page: Three iridized glass banks—the Eagle and Star, the Wise Owl, and the Liberty Bell—produced by the Anchor Hocking Company

# New Carnival Glass

New Carnival glass—comprising new issues, specialty items, and reproductions—has been produced since 1962. According to its manufacturers, the new glass is being made in essentially the same way that the old glass was. Certainly, some of the old molds are being used again. These reissues and reproductions of the old glass enable today's collector to obtain copies of some of the famous old Carnival ware as well as the new glass now being made, which may well become the collector's items of the future.

Most of today's companies are marking their new glass to prevent it from being mistaken for the old. However, unscrupulous dealers have been known to grind off or otherwise deface these marks. To avoid difficulty, buy your Carnival glass from a reputable dealer, and familiarize yourself with what is being made in New Carnival glass today.

New Carnival glass already has its own very personal history, starting with the Imperial Glass Company's reissue of the Imperial's Grape goblet in 1962. The Fenton Art Glass Company put out their first new collection in 1969, followed by the St. Clair Glass Works, the Indiana Glass Company, the L. E. Smith Glass Company, Elizabeth Degenhart of the Crystal Art Glass Company, and the Hansen Brothers of Michigan. Other manufacturers that have produced the New Carnival glass are the Federal Glass Company, the

---

Facing page: A pitcher and goblets in the New Carnival glass pattern Harvest, first produced by the Indiana Glass Company in the 1970s

Westmoreland Glass Company, the Jeannette Glass Company, and the Wheaton-Nuline Company.

## THE IMPERIAL GLASS COMPANY

The Imperial Glass Company of Bellaire, Ohio, founded in 1902, was one of the original makers of Carnival glass. They began production for a new line of Carnival glass in 1962 with the Imperial's Grape goblet. Imperial has now become one of the largest manufacturers of the new iridized glass. Many of their pieces are reissues of their old patterns. They have marked all the new glass with the trademark IG. The colors that Imperial has made in the new glass are Rubigold, Peacock, Sunset Ruby, Amber, White, Azure Blue, Cobalt Blue, and Helios Green. All except Amber and White have been discontinued. The Aurora Jewels pattern in Cobalt Blue and Helios Green, produced in smaller quantities than other discontinued colors, are now considered quite collectible.

In 1969 Imperial started to produce limited edition plates. This series was called America the Beautiful. It was followed in 1970 by the Twelve Days of Christ-

New Carnival glass salt-and-pepper shakers by Imperial: Salz and Pfeffer on the left, and Imperial's Grape on the right

The Mount Rushmore plate from Imperial's limited edition series America the Beautiful (1970)

Covered butter dish, sugar, and creamer in a reissued Imperial pattern: Lustre Rose

Three limited edition plates by Fenton: Mother's Day (1971), American Craftsman (1973), and Christmas in America (1970)

mas, a series which will be completed in 1982 and features one day of Christmas each year. These plates are also very collectible. Some of the reissued Imperial patterns are Pansy, Lustre Rose, and Imperial's Grape.

## THE FENTON ART GLASS COMPANY

The Fenton Art Glass Company of Williamstown, West Virginia, founded in 1905, was another of the original manufacturers of Carnival Glass that have started making new glass. They started production in 1969 and state that they are using the old formulas for iridizing glass. Their new pieces are quite extensive, including limited editions, commemorative items, and new patterns and shapes, as well as many reissues of their old glass. The Fenton Company now owns the old Northwood molds as well, and their reissues are of both their own and Northwood patterns. Fenton's new pieces are all embossed with the company's name.

Many series of limited edition plates have also been produced by Fenton, including Christmas in America,

The American Craftsman, and Mother's Day plates. In 1972 they issued a marigold Famous Lovers plate, a proposed series made for the Kensington Glass Company. However, the only one made before the series was discontinued was the Romeo and Juliet plate. Fenton has also made commemorative items for the Bicentennial year. Other decorative pieces are being made in the New Carnival glass in marigold, orange, purple, and blue, although not all patterns are made in all colors.

## THE ST. CLAIR GLASS WORKS

The St. Clair Glass Works of Elwood, Indiana, was founded in 1938. The St. Clair brothers started producing New Carnival glass in the 1960s. Among the first items they made was an Indian head toothpick holder which has since become a collector's item. In 1972 the company was sold to Richard Gregg. However, Joe St. Clair still makes New Carnival glass at his Joe St. Clair Glass Works. His products include paperweights, doorstops, toothpick holders, and other whimseys. Most of his pieces are marked with his name or his initials.

Toothpick holders by the St. Clair Glass Works: Indian Head, Swan, Bicentennial, Owl, and Cactus

### THE INDIANA GLASS COMPANY
The Indiana Glass Company, Dunkirk, Indiana, was founded in 1904, and first started producing the new iridized glass in 1971. They produced inexpensive glassware in quantity without a trademark. Their pieces are mass-produced and widely distributed. They make a group of so-called heirloom pieces which are marked with an identifying sticker and are reissues of authentic near-cut designs. They also make a covered hen dish, hostess plates, a Garland compote, and a Harvest series.

### THE L. E. SMITH GLASS COMPANY
The L. E. Smith Glass Company was founded in 1907. They experimented with making New Carnival glass in the 1960s and their first line was produced in 1971. Most of their pieces are marked with an S. They are most famous for their limited edition collector's plates, made in an excellent quality glass, and especially noteworthy in amethyst. They also manufacture other shapes in New Carnival glass in green, amethyst, gold, and crystal lustre, a crystal with a mother-of-pearl finish.

### ELIZABETH DEGENHART
Elizabeth Degenhart of Crystal Art Glass, Cambridge, Ohio, makes glass shapes which are iridized by others —for example, the Hansen Brothers and Joe St. Clair. Mrs. Degenhart produces match holders, toothpick holders, paperweights, vases, cream and sugar sets, and whimseys. Her pieces are of excellent quality and made in limited amounts.

### THE HANSEN BROTHERS
The Hansen brothers, Ronald Hansen of Mackinaw City, Michigan, and Robert Hansen of Bridgeport, Michigan, started working together on their own formulas for iridizing glass in the early 1960s. They do not

Two contemporary pieces: a Hen on Nest by Fenton, and a Hen on Nest by the Indiana Glass Company

Limited edition collector's plates by the L. E. Smith Company: Robert E. Lee (1972), Christmas Plate (1972), and Jefferson Davis (1972)

Covered Swan dish made by the Jeannette Glass Company

Contemporary punch bowl set by the L. E. Smith Company

A planter in the New Carnival glass pattern Mermaid, by Fenton

make the glass they iridize but use glass shapes made by other companies. They also iridize for other people, such as Elizabeth Degenhart. Most of their early pieces have only a pontil mark, while later pieces carry their initials or signatures. The brothers now work independently. Hansen pieces bring top Art glass prices because of their excellent quality and limited quantity.

## THE WHEATON-NULINE COMPANY
The Wheaton-Nuline Company of Millville, New Jersey, has made a series of Wheaton commemorative decanters, produced in limited editions. Not all the decanters are iridized. They come in the following series: Presidential, Great American, Astronaut, Star, and Christmas. Some of the decanters, such as Thomas Jefferson, John F. Kennedy, and F. D. Roosevelt of the Presidential series, are sold out and can only be purchased from other collectors or dealers. Wheaton also makes a series of miniature bottles featuring American presidents from Washington to Nixon. These are not made in limited editions and are generally available.

**Other companies.** Other glass companies also produce iridized glass. The Jeannette Glass Company of Jeannette, Pennsylvania, makes pitcher and tumbler sets and an antique classic series, one of which is a covered swan dish. The Federal Glass Company of Columbus, Ohio, makes milky-white iridescent tableware and beer mugs. The Westmoreland Glass Company of Grapeville, Pennsylvania, has made limited editions of collectors plates. These are the Three Owls, the Three Kittens, the Cherub, the American Indian, and George Washington.

## COLLECTING NEW GLASS
If you wish to collect some of the new pieces being made in Carnival glass today, there are certain items worthy of consideration. Limited editions of all kinds,

Three Wheaton commemorative decanters: Robert Kennedy, from the Great American Series; Abraham Lincoln, Presidential Series; Apollo XI, Astronaut Series; and in the center, two miniature Presidential bottles

especially plates and decanters; souvenir and commemorative glass made with dates, places, and serial numbers; collector's items issued by individuals and associations table sets and other sets of all kinds; experimental items, whimseys, and signed pieces; and miniature items in Carnival glass are among today's collectibles.

Limited editions usually have an embossed date or serial number. Once the last projected number is reached, the molds are destroyed. The limited editions, including collector's plates and commemorative decanters, will increase in value as long as there is a demand for them.

Souvenir and commemorative items are glassware commissioned by individuals or organizations to commemorate an event. The Fenton Art Glass Company reissued the Northwood Grape and Cable humidor to commemorate the Presznick Carnival Glass Museum in Lodi, Ohio. In 1966 the American Carnival Glass Association began commissioning pieces for their annual conventions. The International Carnival Glass Association issued its first commemorative item in 1969, the St. Louis Arch bottle, from the Wheaton-Nuline Company. The quantity and availability of this type of glass are initially controlled by the people who have commissioned them.

Sets of all kinds are usually more valuable than individual shapes. These sets have become as popular in the New Carnival glass as they were in the old. Whimseys, miniatures, paperweights, toothpick holders, and bells are some of the smaller items popular with collectors.

Discontinued items pose a unique problem—there is no way of predicting whether these pieces will remain discontinued. A manufacturer may stop production on a particular item for various reasons: costs may be too high to produce the piece at a good retail price; or a shape, style, or color may not prove popular. If marketing or other considerations change, however, a manufacturer might reissue these previously discontinued pieces.

If you wish to collect in this area, it is wise to check the original selling price and learn what the pieces are currently selling for by checking with dealers, other collectors, or newspaper ads.

# Collecting and Purchasing

There is no right way to collect Carnival glass. What you decide to collect will depend upon your particular interests, the amount of money you wish to spend, and the display and storage areas that you have available. Collect the pieces that bring you the most pleasure. One way to start a collection is to collect either patterns, shapes, or colors—or to collect pieces from an individual manufacturer.

## PATTERN

You might wish to start collecting a particular pattern category which is allied to your interests, such as flowers, animals, or near-cuts. Or collect a favorite design motif, accumulating as many different shapes and colors as possible. For instance, you may want to collect grape patterns. Such a collection could include as many pieces as you can find in Northwood's Grape and Cable, Imperial's Grape, Vintage, and other grape patterns. (If you choose to specialize in only one specific pattern, it will be a challenge to amass all the known shapes, because different shapes were made in different quantities. For instance, Northwood's Grape and Cable was made in over fifty shapes—and many are quite rare.) Or, possibly, collect as many different patterns as appeal to you, owning one or two shapes in as many patterns as possible.

## SHAPE

Collecting according to shape is another good way to start. Collect only vases or bowls in as many patterns

# COLLECTING and PURCHASING

as you can. Some people collect only cream and sugar sets, others collect rosebowls, tumblers, hats, baskets, or whimseys.

## COLOR
A striking collection can be made by choosing only one color, but collecting as many patterns and shapes that can be found in that color. The two most common colors are marigold and purple, the rarest are red and white. The pastels in general are harder to find than the bright, vivid colors.

## MANUFACTURER
An interesting collection could be formed by collecting pieces from only one manufacturer. In Northwood, you would find Peacock at the Fountain, Peacock and Urn, Grape and Cable, Three Fruits, and Daisy and

Whimseys, like these by Fenton, are popular collectibles.

Plume, to name a few. A Fenton collection would include Persian Medallion, Orange Tree, and Butterfly and Berry. This type of collection may present problems, however, because certain patterns were made by more than one manufacturer—and you may find it difficult to identify the maker of a pattern you like.

## PURCHASING

Once you have decided what to collect, you are faced with the problem of where and how to purchase your Carnival glass. As much knowledge and information as you can obtain before you buy is worth the time spent acquiring it.

If you are hurried or distracted, buying can be difficult. And, of course, you don't want to spend more money than a piece is worth. So learn to recognize the type of glass you are interested in. Visit reliable glass dealers. Examine carefully any piece you are interested in. Learn as much as you can about the execution of details of each piece.

**Damaged pieces.** When purchasing any piece of glass, see if it is perfect or damaged. Only a perfect piece can demand the best price. Check each piece thoroughly for chips and cracks. Carefully run your finger around the top and bottom rims to feel small, hard-to-see chips. Hold the piece up to direct light to detect cracks that may not otherwise be visible. Of course, chips in the base of the piece are not as aesthetically objectionable as those on the upper, outer rim.

Bubbles are frequently seen in Carnival glass. They do not devalue a piece or set a standard of quality. Bubbles only present a problem when they have burst. This occurs when an air bubble rises to the surface and breaks before the piece has cooled, leaving a smooth pockmark or pocket. This often happens in deep pieces with heavy patterns. It is not a serious problem, but the piece must be considered damaged, nonetheless.

# COLLECTING and PURCHASING

Do not buy a piece if the iridescence seems faded. There is nothing that can be done to restore its lustre. Since part of the attraction of Carnival glass is its iridescence and color, a badly faded piece is as damaged and devalued as one with chips and cracks.

Buy a damaged piece only if it is important to you because of its rarity, or if it fills a gap in your collection. It may be possible to repair or restore the piece if it is not too badly damaged (see page 121). If it is intended primarily for display, a small defect may not be too noticeable.

**Where to buy.** Carnival glass may be bought from many sources. A reputable antiques or glass dealer is a good place to start. Often pieces purchased there have been checked for condition and authenticity.

A very popular place to buy Carnival glass is at a flea market. If you arrive at the market early you will find the best selection of merchandise. Antique and collectibles shows are other good places to visit for Carnival glass. You can see what glass is available, and get a general idea of the prices that are being asked for the pieces that you may be interested in.

Other purchasing sources are house sales, barn sales, garage sales, and auctions. At auctions you may handle the glass and also see what prices the items you are interested in bring. Carnival glass may be bought by mail, also. Individuals and dealers often place ads for buying and selling Carnival glass in specialized papers and magazines dealing in antiques and collectibles. Some of these publications are *The Antique Trader Weekly*, *Hobbies* magazine, and *The Antiques Journal*. (For others, see page 124.)

# Care and Display

Old pieces of Carnival glass have survived because they were treated carefully. Most of this glass was not used every day because of its fragile nature. The same caution should apply to Carnival glass today.

## CARE

When washing Carnival glass, avoid harsh detergents and cleaning agents as well as extreme water temperatures. Very hot or very cold water can cause cracks. A weak solution of a mild detergent will make the glassware sparkle. Vinegar or washing soda are good for removing sediment in the bottom of a vase or other closed piece. Fill the glass with a mild solution of either and let stand a day or so. If one of the solutions doesn't work, the other probably will.

Although Carnival glass looks lovely against the sun in a window, this is not the best place for it. Heat checks, or partial cracks, can occur when glass has been exposed to great changes of temperature in a short time, and this can happen to glassware left on a windowsill where the temperature drops sharply from morning to night.

In addition, the ultraviolet rays of the sun can discolor a clear piece of glass if either manganese or selenium were added to the glass formula. These agents were used to keep the base glass from turning aqua. Eventually, manganese will produce a violet cast and selenium an amber cast. The intensity of the color change depends on the amount of the chemical that has been added and the length of time the glass has remained in the sun. This can take years to happen to any perceptible degree. The iridescent portion of the glass will not be affected, only the clear base glass.

## REPAIR

If a piece has been badly broken, it is advisable to have it repaired professionally, especially if the piece is valuable. A professional restorer has the proper tools available for restoration. Grinding and polishing by an expert can remove small nicks and chips. Remember, however, that even with the best of care, glass can be damaged in the process. If a piece is not too badly broken, you may be able to mend it yourself with the new transparent epoxy cements that are now available.

## DISPLAY

Carnival glass looks best when displayed in a good light source. Very often a collection is shown in a closed cabinet with glass doors and sides where the shelves are lit with concealed bulbs. However, Carnival glass need not be enclosed; it can be displayed in most areas of the home effectively.

Carnival glass arrangements may be displayed against a background of modern furniture. Metal and glass shelves can hold a collection of Carnival glass. A grouping of dark Carnival pieces are attractive on a clear glass or acrylic coffee or end table. The bright colors and heavy iridescence of Carnival glass provide contrast in a setting that is monochromatic, neutral, or white.

Rather than amassing an extensive collection of Carnival glass, you may only want to own several pieces of the glass to hold flowers, fruits, and candies, just as they were used in the households of the early 1900s.

To get the most pleasure from your Carnival glass, use it in any way that appeals to you and that you feel enhances its inherent quality.

# Glossary

**Art glass**—an expensive hand-blown glassware, featuring unusual effects of color, shape, and design. These pieces were usually ornamental, but some utilitarian objects were also made. American Art glass was most popular during the 1880s through the early 1900s.

**Base color**—the color of the glass used for Carnival ware before the iridescence is applied.

**Carnival glass**—a colored, pressed glassware with a fired-on iridescent finish, made in the United States from about 1905 to 1925.

**Cut glass**—glass, usually a heavy flint glass, which has been decorated by cutting geometric patterns into the glass with grinding wheels and abrasives, and then smoothing and polishing the resultant designs. This method of decorating glass originated in Germany and was first introduced into the United States from England in the late eighteenth century.

**Depression glass**—an inexpensive, machine-made, mass-produced glassware for dinner sets and giftware which was produced in a variety of colors from about 1920 to 1940. It was also sometimes iridized.

**Fired-on iridescence**—giving an iridescent finish to glass by adding metallic salts, after which the glass is refired.

**Flashed-on iridescence**—adding a thin, allover iridescent coating by dipping hot glass into a solution of metallic salts.

**Hand-blown glass**—glass formed and shaped with a blowpipe and other hand-manipulated tools, without the use of molds.

**Iridescence**—a sparkling rainbow-colored quality given to glass by the addition of metallic salts.

**Iridized**—coated with iridescence.

**Molded glass**—glass which has been given its partial or final shape by being blown into a mold, called mold blown, or by being pressed into a mold by machine.

**Near-cut**—pressed glass patterns which imitate the designs of hand-decorated cut glass.

**New Carnival glass**—an iridescent colored glass, which includes new issues, specialty items, and reproductions, that has been made since 1962 in essentially the same way that the original Carnival glass was made, and in some cases utilizing the original molds.

**Opalescence**—a milky or cloudy quality given to glass by the addition of tin or zinc.

**Pattern glass**—glass mechanically pressed into a variety of designs and shapes. There are more than 2,000 patterns and variants of this American tableware which was popular during the period from 1840 to 1900.

**Pressed glass**—glass formed by a mechanical process in which hot glass is forced into molds under pressure and removed in an almost finished state. Pressed glass was an American invention introduced in the 1820s.

**Sprayed-on iridescence**—adding iridescence to glass by spraying it with particles of metallic salts.

**Whimsey**—a small, unusual, decorative glass object made to display an individual glassmaker's skill.

# Bibliography

Hand, Sherman, *Colors in Carnival Glass*, Volumes 1-4. Sherman Hand, 8819 42nd Ave. S.W., Seattle, Washington, 1967-72.

———*New 1975 Price Guide of Carnival Glass*. Sherman Hand, 8819 42nd Ave. S.W., Seattle, Washington, 1975.

Hartung, Marion T., *Carnival Glass in Color*. Marion T. Hartung, Box 69, Emporia, Kansas, 1967.

———*Carnival Glass Series*, Books 1-10, 2nd edition. Marion T. Hartung, Box 69, Emporia, Kansas, 1968.

———*Northwood Pattern Glass in Color*. Marion T. Hartung, Box 69, Emporia, Kansas, 1969.

Klamkin, Marion, *The Collector's Guide to Depression Glass*. Hawthorn Books, Inc., New York, New York, 1973.

Lee, Ruth Webb, *Handbook of Early American Pressed Glass Patterns*. Lee Publications, Wellesley Hills, Massachusetts, 1974.

Linn, Alan, *The Fenton Story of Glass Making*. Fenton Art Glass Company, Williamstown, West Virginia, 1969.

Lowe, Mrs. Lucille, "Notes from the Millersburg Museum." *Antique Trader Annual of Articles for 1973*, Dubuque, Iowa, 1973.

McKearin, George S. and Helen, *American Glass*. Crown Publishers, New York, New York, 1941.

Presznick, Rose M., *Carnival and Iridescent Glass with Price Guide*, Books 1-4. Rose M. Presznick, Lodi, Ohio, 1966.

———*Presznick's Encyclopedia of New Carnival and Iridescent Glass*. Rose M. Presznick, Lodi, Ohio, 1974.

Revi, Albert Christian, *American Pressed Glass and Figure Bottles*. Thomas Nelson and Sons, New York, New York, 1964.

## Publications

*The Antiques Journal*
P.O. Box 1046
Dubuque, Iowa 52001

*The Antique Trader Weekly*
P.O. Box #1050
Dubuque, Iowa, 52001

*Hobbies*, the Magazine for Collectors
1006 South Michigan Ave.
Chicago, Illinois, 60605

## Clubs

International Carnival Glass Association
Department A-T
R. R. 2
Warren, Indiana, 46792

American Carnival Glass Association
Lakewood, Ohio, 44107

# Index

**Boldface** page numbers indicate illustrations.

American Carnival Glass Association, 115
American Craftsman (series; Fenton), **108**, 109
American Indian (Westmoreland), 113
America the Beautiful (series; Imperial), 106, **107**
Anchor Hocking Company, **102**, 103
Anniversary (Jeannette), 101
Art glass, 4, 8–9, 16, 122
Astronaut (series; Wheaton-Nuline), 113, **114**

Basketweave (Northwood; secondary pattern), 23, 42, 46, 71, 78
Basketweave Variant, 90, **91**
Beaded Basket, 84, **85**
Beaded Bull's-eye, 26, **33**
Beads (Northwood), **38**, 40
Bearded Berry (Fenton; secondary pattern), 23, 51
Beauty Bud, **24**, 26
Bicentennial (St. Clair), **109**
Bouquet and Lattice see Normandie
Bugeye, 94, **95**
Bumblebees, 90, **91**
Butterfly (or Scarab), 90, **91**
Butterfly and Berry (Fenton), 10, 57, **59**, 118; secondary pattern, 58

Cactus (St. Clair), **109**
Cambridge Glass Company, 14–15, 23
Canada Dry, 78, **79**, 81
Carder, Frederick, 4, 9
care, 120
Carnival Holly, 20, 93, **95**
Cattails, 90, **91**
Cherry (Fenton), 20
Cherub (Westmoreland), 113
Christmas (series; Wheaton-Nuline), 113

Christmas in America (series; Fenton), 108, **108**
Cleveland Memorial (Millersburg), 13
Coin Dot, **17**, 40, **41**
collecting and purchasing, 5, 15, 116–19; New Carnival glass, 105, 113–15
color, 10, 13, 16–18, 19, 117; later glass, 97, 98; New Carnival glass, 106, 109, 110
commemoratives, 25, 39; New Carnival glass, 108, 109, 113, 114–15
Continental Distilling Corporation, **79**, 81
Corning Glass Company, 94, **95**
Courthouse (Millersburg), 13, 20
Covered Hen, **92**, 93
Crackle, **24**, 29, 88, **89**
Craquelle (Venetian Frosted), 88
Crystal Art Glass Company, 105, 110
Crystal Glass Ltd., 44, **45**
Curved Star, 72, **73**

Daisy and Plume (Northwood), **66**, 67, 117–18
damages and repair, 118–19, 121
Degenhart, Elizabeth, 105, 110, 113
Depression glass, 97–103
Diamond (Millersburg), 14, **76**, 77
Diamond Lace, 20, **38**, 40
Diamond Point (Northwood), **28**, 29
Diamond Point and Fine Rib, **28**, 29
Diamond Ring, **38**, 40
Double Dutch, 20, 57, **60**
Dragon and Lotus (Fenton), **38**, 40
Dunbar Glass Company, 98

Famous Lovers (series; Fenton), 109
Fashion, 20; Imperial, **21**, 72, **73**
Federal Glass Company, 98–100, 99, 105, 113
Fenton Art Glass Company, 4, 10–11, 16, 17, 22–23; Bearded Berry (secondary pattern), 23, 51; Butterfly and Berry, 10, 57, **59**, 118; Butterfly and Berry (secondary pattern), 58; Cherry, 20; Dragon and Lotus, **38**, 40; Fenton's Basket,

84, **85**; Fish Scale (secondary pattern), 94; Floral and Grape, 74, **75**; Grape and Cable, 20, 42, **43**; Grape Leaves and Acorns, 42; Long Thumbprints, **34**, 35; Orange Tree, 10, **11**, 55, 94, **95**, 118; Panther, 58, **59**; Peacock and Grape, **48**, 51; Persian Medallion, 10, **21**, 22, 23, 51, 118; Rustic, **27**, 35; Stag and Holly, 58, **60**; Thistle, **22**, **61**, 62; Waterlily and Cattails (secondary pattern), 62; Wide Panel (secondary pattern), 58

Fenton Art Glass Company — New Carnival glass, 23, 105, 108–09; American Craftsman (series), **108**, 109; Christmas in America (series), 108, **108**; Famous Lovers (series), 109; Fruits and Flowers, 71; Hen on Nest, **111**; Mermaid, **112**; Mother's Day (series), **108**, 109; Northwood patterns reissued, 23, 108, 115

Fenton's Basket (Fenton), 84, **85**

Fine Cut in Ovals (Millersburg; secondary pattern), 52

Fine Rib, 22, 29, **31**, 62; Imperial (secondary pattern), 35; Northwood, 29, **31**

Fine Rib Fan, **24**, 30

Fish Scale (Fenton; secondary pattern), 94

Floral and Grape (Fenton), 74, **75**

Four Flowers, **15**, 83

Frog, 93, **95**

Fruits and Flowers: Fenton, 71; Northwood, **70**, 71

Golden Wedding, **80**, 81

Grape and Cable: Fenton, 20, 42, **43**; Northwood, 14, 20, 42, **43**, **86**, 87, 93, **95**, 116, 117; Northwood, Fenton reissue, 115

Grape Arbor, 20; Northwood, **86**, 87

Grape Cluster, 20

Grape Delight, **12**, 20, 67

Grape Leaves and Acorns: Fenton, 42; Millersburg, 42, **43**

Great American (series; Wheaton-Nuline), 113, **114**

Handbag, **92**, 93

Hansen Brothers, 105, 110, 113

Harvest (Indiana), **104**, 110

Heisey Glass Company, 15, 23

Hemingray Glass Company, 94, **95**

Hen on Nest: Fenton, **111**; Indiana, 110, **111**

Hobnail, 30, **33**

Hobnail Swirl (Millersburg), 14, **27**, 30

Imperial Glass Company, 4, 11, 13, 16, 22, 23, 106; Fashion, **21**, 72, **73**; Fine Rib (secondary pattern), 35; Imperial's Grape, 13, 20, **24**, **43**, 45, **76**, 77, 116; Imperial's Grape, reissue, 105, 106, **106**, 108; Lustre Rose, 13, 58, **59**, **75**, 77; Lustre Rose, reissue, **107**, 108; Mayflower, **92**, 94; Open Rose, 20, **21**, 46; Open Rose, reissue, 46; Pansy, 20, 46, **47**, 68, **69**; Pansy, reissue, 108; Peacock Tail, **49**, 51; Quilted Diamonds (secondary pattern), 46, 68; Ripple, **34**, 35; Smooth Rib (secondary pattern), 77; Twins, **54**, 55; Wide Panel (secondary pattern), 51

Imperial Glass Company – New Carnival glass, 13, 23, 105, 106, 108; America the Beautiful (series), 106, **107**; Cambridge and Heisey molds used, 23; Imperial's Grape, 105, 106, **106**, 108; Lustre Rose, 107, 108; Open Rose, 46; Pansy, 108; Salz and Pfeffer, **106**; Twelve Days of Christmas (series), 106, 108

Imperial's Grape (Imperial), 13, 20, **24**, **43**, 45, **76**, 77, 116; reissue, 105, 106, **106**, 108

Indiana Glass Company, 15, **104**, 105, 110, **111**

Indian Head (St. Clair), 109, **109**

International Carnival Glass Association, 115

iridescence, 18–19, 119, 122, 123; later glass, 97, 98

Iris and Herringbone (Jeannette), 100, **100**

# INDEX 127

Jack-in-the-Pulpit, 30, **32**
Jeannette Glass Company, 100–01, **100**, **101**, 103, 105, **112**, 113
Jenkins Glass Company, 15; Sunflower Diamond, **33**, 35

Kensington Glass Company, 109
Knotted Beads, 30, **34**
Kookaburra Bird (Crystal Glass Ltd.), **44**, 45

late Carnival glass, 97, 98, 100–01, 103
Lea, 72, **73**
Leaf and Beads (Northwood), 20, **56**, 57
Leaf Rays, 20, 68, **69**
Lined Lattice, 30, **33**, 35
Long Thumbprints (Fenton), **34**, 35
Louisa (Jeannette), 100–01, **101**
Lustre Flute (Northwood), **86**, 87
Lustre Rose, 20; Imperial, 13, 58, **59**, **75**, 77; Imperial, reissue, **107**, 108

Madrid (Federal), 99–100
marks, 14, 22, 23; New Carnival glass, 23, 105, 106, 108, 110, 113, 115
Mayflower, 20; Imperial, **92**, 94
Millersburg Glass Company, 4, 13–14, 22–23; Cleveland Memorial, 13; Courthouse, 13, 20; Diamond, 14, **76**, 77; Fine Cut in Ovals (secondary pattern), 52; Grape Leaves and Acorns, 42, **43**; Hobnail Swirl, 14, **27**, 30; Nesting Swan, 14; Whirling Leaves, 14, 52, **53**; Wide Panel (secondary pattern), 42
Mother's Day (series; Fenton), **108**, 109

Nesting Swan (Millersburg), 14
New Carnival glass, 5, 23, 105–115
Nippon, 22; Northwood, 46, **47**
Normandie (or Bouquet and Lattice; Federal), 98–99, **99**
Northwood Glass Company, 4, 14, 17, 22-23; Basketweave (secondary pattern), 23, 42, 46, 71, 78; Beads, **38**, 40; Daisy and Plume, **66**, 67, 117–18; Diamond Point, **28**, 29; Fenton reissues of Northwood patterns, 23, 108, 115; Fine Rib, 29, **31**; Fruits and Flowers, **70**, 71; Grape and Cable, 14, 20, 42, **43**, **86**, 87, 93, **95**, 116, 117; Grape and Cable, Fenton reissue, 115; Grape Arbor, **86**, 87; Leaf and Beads, 20, **56**, 57; Lustre Flute, **86**, 87; Nippon, 46, **47**; Oriental Poppy, 77, **79**; Peacock and Urn, 20, 117; Peacock at the Fountain, 14, 20, 58, **60**, 117; Plume and Snowflake (secondary pattern), 23, 42; Poppy, 20, **47**, 51; Raspberry, 78, **79**; Raspberry (secondary pattern), 67; Singing Birds, 78, **79**; Stippled Ray, **50**, 52; Thin Rib, **24**, 36, **37**; Thin Rib Variant, 36, **37**; Three Fruits, 6, **62**, 71, 117; Thumbprint (secondary pattern), 23, 87; Tree Trunk, **27**, 36; Wild Rose, 62, **63**

Open Rose (Imperial), 20, **21**, 46; reissue, 46
Orange Tree (Fenton), 10, **11**, 55, 94, **95**, 118
Oriental Poppy (Northwood), 77, **79**
Owl (St. Clair), **109**

Painted Cherries, **76**, 78
Pansy (Imperial), 20, 46, **47**, 68, **69**; reissue, 108
Panther, 20; Fenton, 58, **59**
pattern, 19–20, 22, 116; later glass, 98; New Carnival glass, 108; secondary pattern, 23, 39
Peach and Pear, 20, 46, **48**
Peacock and Grape (Fenton), **48**, 51
Peacock and Urn (Northwood), 20, 117
Peacock at the Fountain (Northwood), 14, 20, 58, **60**, 117
Peacock Tail (Imperial), **49**, 51
Persian Medallion (Fenton), 10, **21**, 22, 23, 51, 118
Pineapple, 72, **73**

Pinwheel, 90, **91**
Plume and Snowflake (Northwood; secondary pattern), 23, 42
Poppy (Northwood), 20, **47**, 51
Presidential (series; Wheaton-Nuline), 113, **114**
Pulled Loop, **33**, 35

Question Marks, **70**, 71
Quilted Diamonds (Imperial; secondary pattern), 46, 68

Raspberry (Northwood), 78, **79**; secondary pattern, 67
repair, 121
Ripple (Imperial), **34**, 35
Robin, 20
Rustic (Fenton), **27**, 35

St. Clair Glass Works, 105, 109, **109**
St. Clair, Joe, 109, 110
Scotch Thistle, 20, **64**, 65
shape, 9, 25, 116–17; New Carnival glass, 115
Ship and Stars, **82**, 83
Singing Birds, 20; Northwood, 78, **79**
Smith Glass Company, L. E., 105, 110, **111, 112**
Smooth, **64**, 65
Smooth Rib, **18**, 51; Imperial (secondary pattern), 77
Soda Gold, 88, **89**
Stag and Holly, 20; Fenton, 58, **60**
Star (series; Wheaton-Nuline), 113
Star and File, 20, **70**, 71
Star Medallion, **49**, 52, 74, **75**
Stippled Flower, **15**, 52
Stippled Ray, 22, **64**, 65; Northwood, **50**, 52
Stork and Rushes, **76**, 78
Sunflower Diamond (Jenkins), **33**, 35

Swan: Jeannette, **112**, 113; St. Clair, 109

Thin Rib (Northwood), **24**, 36, **37**
Thin Rib Variant (Northwood), 36, **37**
Thistle (Fenton), **22**, **61**, 62
Thistle and Thorn, 74, **75**
Three Fruits, 20; Northwood, **6**, 62, 71, 117
Three Kittens (Westmoreland), 113
Three Owls (Westmoreland), 113
Thumbprint (Northwood; secondary pattern), 23, 87
Tiffany, Louis Comfort, 4, 8–9
Top o' the Morning, 90, **91**
Tree of Life, 88
Tree Trunk (Northwood), **27**, 36
Twelve Days of Christmas (series; Imperial), 106, 108
Twins, 20; Imperial, **54**, 55

Veiling, 90, **91**
Venetian Frosted (Craquelle), 88
Venetian Thread, 84, **85**
Vintage, 20, **49**, 52, 64, **65**, 116

Waterlily and Cattails (Fenton; secondary pattern), 62
Westmoreland Glass Company, 105, 113
Wheaton-Nuline Company, 105, 113, **114**, 115
Whirling Leaves (Millersburg), 14, 52, **53**
Wide Panel, 22, **86**, 88; Fenton (secondary pattern), 58; Imperial (secondary pattern), 51; Millersburg (secondary pattern), 42; secondary pattern, 52
Wild Rose (Northwood), 62, **63**
Woodpecker, **24**, 36